Network Models of the Diffusion of Innovations

Quantitative Methods in Communication

George A. Barnett, Editor

Network Models of the Diffusion of Innovations
Thomas W. Valente

forthcoming

WORDij: Automatic Content Analysis of Text
James Danowski

Persuason: Advances through Meta-Analysis
Mike Allen and Raymond W. Preiss, eds.

Network Models of the Diffusion of Innovations

Thomas W. Valente
The John Hopkins University

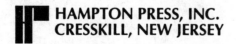
HAMPTON PRESS, INC.
CRESSKILL, NEW JERSEY

Printed in the United States of America

Library of Congress Cataloging-in-Publication Data

Valente, Thomas W.
    Network models of the diffusion of innovations / Thomas W.
Valente.
        p.   cm. -- (The Hampton Press communication series.
Quantitative methods in communication)
    Includes bibliographical references and indexes.
    ISBN 1-881303-21-7. -- ISBN 1-881303-22-5
    1. Diffusion of innovations. 2. Network analysis (Planning)
I. Title. II. Series.
HC79.T4V35   1994
338.9'26--dc20   94-24387
                                                              CIP

Hampton Press, Inc.
23 Broadway
Cresskill, NJ 07626

DEDICATION
To 'Becca:

Live hand in hand
And together we'll stand
On the threshold of a dream
(Moody Blues, 1969)

Contents

Acknowledgments

The present volume benefited from the aid, support, and encouragement provided by Professor Everett M. Rogers during my graduate school years (at the Annenberg School for Communication, USC) and now in my professional career). I also received considerable intellectual help from Philip Bonacich, Ronald M. Rice, and George A. Barnett. Special thanks to my colleagues at the Center for Communication Programs, Johns Hopkins University, including Larry Kincaid and Robert Foreman, whose Gauss expertise made me realize what a dinosaur I really am.

Numerous colleagues such as Mark Granovetter, Bill Loges, David Waterman, Mary Ann Pentz, William Dutton, and anonymous journal reviewers have provided feedback on various pieces of this research. My parents and family deserve special thanks for their kind words of encouragement and support.

Rebecca Davis deserves special credit for helping to clarify many of the topics discussed here.

Foreword

For the past half century, since the publication of the Iowa hybrid corn study by Bryce Ryan and Neal C. Gross in 1943, diffusion scholars have sought to explain why the rate of adoption of an innovation starts out slowly, but then, at 10% or 20% or 25% adoption by the members of a system, suddenly takes off, so that in the next few time periods almost everyone in the system has adopted. When viewed over time, an innovation's rate of adoption thus looks like an S-curve.

A first step in understanding this mystery was to realize that the diffusion of an innovation is a social process, in which individuals adopt the new idea as the result of talking with other individuals who have already adopted. Ryan and Gross hinted at this social nature of the diffusion process when they found that "friends and neighbors" were reported by Iowa farmers as the most important source/channel of communication in convincing them to adopt the hybrid seed. But Ryan and Gross did not know more specifically exactly which other farmers in their two Iowa communities of study talked with an individual respondent about hybrid seed corn (Valente & Rogers, 1993).

Sociometric questions were asked of the medical doctor respondents in a study of the diffusion of tetracycline in four Illinois communities by James S. Coleman, Herbert Menzel, and Elihu Katz in the mid-1950s. Here was more definitive evidence of the social nature of the diffusion of an innovation. The three Columbia University sociologists obtained who-to-whom network data from their physicians, and they performed certain types of rudimentary network analyses to better understand the diffusion process. But sophisticated computer programs to handle the data overload problems of analyzing network data were not available in the 1950s, nor was conceptual thinking about network behavior very advanced. Social science research mainly utilizes the individual as the unit of analysis, a level of investigation that is not very satisfactory in studying networks, in which the relationships between two or more individuals, not the individuals themselves or their personal characteristics, are important.

Tom Valente reanalyzes the medical drug diffusion dataset here, in order to test certain notions about thresholds and the critical mass. He also utilizes two datasets from earlier diffusion studies in Brazil and in Korea in which I was involved. Dr. Valente thus makes a unique contribution to advancing network thinking about the diffusion of innovations. I believe that thresholds and the critical mass offer important conceptual advances in understanding the role of networks in diffusion.

Tom Valente came to this point through a novel intellectual ancestry. After earning his B.S. degree in Mathematics, Tom studied for his M.S. in Mass Communication at San Diego State University with Professor Dave Dozier, who had reanalyzed the Korean dataset on the diffusion of family planning innovations among village women in 1973, in his Ph.D. dissertation at Stanford, where I was then teaching. So, when Tom Valente arrived at the USC Annenberg School for Communication in 1987, he had the ideal academic pedigree for advancing network thinking about diffusion. His Ph.D. dissertation at USC in 1991 was a first step in this direction, then carried forward during his two years of further research at The Johns Hopkins University.

I feel that Tom Valente's novel promise is here fulfilled. The present volume, Network Models of the Diffusion of Innovations, takes network philosophy into new ground. Further steps are expected, perhaps to be taken by scholars who are influenced by Tom's work. Thus is the cumulative nature of science.

Everett M. Rogers
Professor and Chair
University of New Mexico
Albuquerque, NM

Preface

Products, fads, and opinions from hula hoops to new computer technology spread throughout society. Usually, the rate of their spread and the specification of who will adopt when is unknown and unpredictable except in hindsight, as exemplified by this quote:

> Audrey Ashby, a company spokeswoman, acknowledged that the company had been unprepared. "The orders did exceed our expectations," she said. "We had estimated fewer orders because we just weren't quite sure how quickly the product would take off."—New York Times, December 17, 1992

This book presents a key to understanding how ideas, products, opinions, and other things "take off" and spread throughout society, and provides a better means to estimate how fast or slow that spread occurs. The spread of ideas, opinions, and products is referred to as the *diffusion of innovations.*

The diffusion of innovations occurs among individuals in a social system, and the pattern of communication among these individuals is a social network. The network of communication determines how quickly innovations diffuse and the timing for each individual's adoption. The present book analyzes how social networks structure the diffusion of innovations.

Network models of diffusion yield tipping points in the process that are studied through threshold and critical mass models. Threshold models focus on individuals, whereas critical mass models describe social systems. Thresholds and the critical mass, in the context of network models of diffusion, provide a comprehensive picture of how social systems determine social change both for individuals and societies.

Chapter 1 reviews diffusion of innovations theory, network analysis, and the datasets used as examples. Three diffusion datasets are analyzed: (a) the medical innovation study by Coleman, Katz and Menzel (1966), (b) the Brazilian farmers study by Rogers and others (1970), and (c) the Korean family planning study by Rogers and Kincaid (1981). Chapter 2 provides a review of prior research conducted on threshold and critical mass models. Prior research has been conducted in fields such as epidemiology, geography, collective behavior, social movements, economics, and communication technology.

Chapter 3 presents relational network models of diffusion which posit that individuals adopt innovations based on their direct relations with others in their social system. Opinion leadership is a relational model which posits that individuals are influenced by opinion leaders to adopt certain opinions and behaviors. Other relational diffusion models include network density, personal network radiality, and group membership.

Chapter 4 provides structural network models of diffusion which posit that individuals adopt innovations based on their position in the social system, regardless of direct ties to specific others. Structural models differ from relational models in that all relations in the network are considered, not just the behavior of those to whom an individual is directly connected. Structural models also describe the behavior of whole social systems by considering the structure of the network within which diffusion occurs (e.g., diffusion occurs more rapidly in more dense networks). This book reviews structural models such as individual and network centrality, density, and structural equivalence. Empirical conclusions from both relational and structural models are drawn.

Threshold and critical mass models of diffusion are presented in Chapters 5 and 6, respectively. Thresholds are individual measures of the degree of interpersonal influence necessary for someone to adopt an innovation. The social network threshold perspective provided in this volume introduces the notion that individuals may be innovative with respect to their personal network, as well as with respect to the social system.

The critical mass models presented in Chapter 6 show that past research has defined the critical mass in numerous ways. Competing definitions and a lack of clarity in critical mass research has hindered theoretical development of critical mass models. The empirical results presented in Chapter 6 show that a critical mass exists and can be measured in network terms.

Chapter 7 develops a general threshold model of adoption based on social networks. The network threshold model can be conceptualized in both relational and structural terms and provides a general model that more accurately measures individual innovativeness. With the network threshold model, individual innovativeness can be measured relative to an individual's personal network or relative to his or her whole social system. The network threshold model can be used to (a) predict diffusion, (b) identify opinion leaders, (c) understand the two-step flow model of opinion formation, and (d) determine the critical mass.

This book is addressed to researchers, policymakers, and students interested in diffusion of innovations or network analysis. It is also addressed to individuals interested in studying the process of social change as represented by a diffusion/network paradigm. Finally, individuals interested in developing, evaluating, or understanding communication campaigns and media effects can use these concepts to improve their work.

The analysis in this book was greatly facilitated by some excellent software programs. The statistics and some graphs were performed with Stata (Computing Resource Center, 1991). The network threshold model was created with the matrix language program Gauss (Aptech, 1991), which I also used to create other network measures and along with SNAPS (Friedkin, 1989), this program provided the centrality measures. The network graphs were created with GNET (Mellot, 1991), which also uses Gauss (Aptech, 1992). Finally, Excel (Microsoft, 1991) was used to create some of the line graphs.

The social network approach developed in this book originated as my dissertation and benefited from the help and guidance of my graduate faculty. Additionally, portions of this research were submitted to various journals and I greatly benefited from the reviews provided by the *American Journal of Sociology*, *American Sociological Review*, and *Public Opinion Quarterly*. Although I often disagreed with many reviewer comments, more often they provided valuable advice and excellent feedback. Part of the problem is that one paper (without sufficient supporting documents and references) cannot capture all the materials presented in this volume. In fact one reviewer remarked, "expand it to textbook length, however, and I'd seriously consider adopting it for my class." For this reviewer and anyone interested in the diffusion of innovations: Here it is.

Introduction

This book presents network models of the diffusion of innovations and demonstrates how social structure—who communicates with whom—determines the spread of influence, ideas, and products. Three diffusion datasets provide empirical support and examples for the book and use individuals as the unit of analysis. The datasets are: (a) medical doctors prescribing a new drug, (b) Brazilian farmers adopting hybrid corn, and (c) Korean women adopting family planning. The approach can also be applied to the diffusion of innovations among cities, states, or organizations.

This book combines and applies the network approach to the study of the diffusion of innovations in the tradition of two other volumes that have addressed this topic: *Medical Innovation: The Diffusion of a New Drug* (Coleman, Katz, & Menzel, 1966), and *Communication Networks: Toward a new Paradigm for Research* (Rogers & Kincaid, 1981). A third volume, *Micromotives & Macrobehavior* (Schelling, 1978), provided an analysis of threshold and critical mass topics but avoided both network analysis and diffusion of innovations. Threshold and critical mass effects constitute exciting dynamic processes postulated to influence the success or failure of many social-change processes.

Consequently, threshold and critical mass models are given special attention within the diffusion network context. Threshold and critical mass models have received considerable attention in the popular and academic literature, yet their exact specification (definition, operationalization, or analysis) has been avoided. Testing and analyses of threshold and critical mass models has been avoided because few people have had access to the network and diffusion models needed to specify and test threshold and critical mass effects.

DIFFUSION OF INNOVATIONS AND NETWORK ANALYSIS

Diffusion of innovations is the spread of new ideas, opinions, or products throughout a society. "Diffusion is the process by which an innovation is communicated through certain channels over time among the members of a social system" (Rogers, 1983, p. 5; Beal & Bohlen, 1955). Thus, diffusion is a communication process in which adopters persuade those who have not yet adopted to adopt.

Network analysis is a technique used to analyze the pattern of interpersonal communication in a social system by determining who talks to whom. Network analysis can be used to understand the flow of personal influence by enabling researchers to define who influences whom in a social system.

Diffusion of innovations and network analysis have complemented one another for over 30 years. Diffusion of innovations research has been greatly enhanced by network analysis because it permits more exact specification of who influences whom during the diffusion process. Network analysis has benefited from diffusion research by providing a real-world application to compare and clarify network models.

An early and influential study of diffusion was carried out by Ryan and Gross (1943; see also Pemberton, 1936, 1937) who studied the diffusion of hybrid corn among farmers in two Iowa communities. They wanted to know why some farmers adopted this new corn earlier than others and what influenced those adoption decisions. Ryan and Gross showed that the diffusion of an innovation was a social process by reasoning as follows: If all individuals in a social system act as rational economic decision makers, adoption of an advantageous technical innovation should occur for everyone at about the same time. The presence of a substantial length of time between the first and last adopters indicates that social structural and sociopsychological factors influence the process of the diffusion of innovations. The social nature of adoption and diffusion was partly captured by Ryan and Gross (1943, 1950) with variables such as social participation, education, cosmopoliteness, and media consumption. These variables were more highly correlated with innovativeness, as measured by time of adoption, than economic variables such as size of farm and number of years farming.

Figure 1.1 graphs the diffusion of hybrid seed corn among farmers in two Iowa communities from the Ryan and Gross (1943) study. At first, only a few farmers buy the new corn, but as time progresses more and more farmers buy the new corn until some point (here 10 years) when all eligible farmers have adopted hybrid corn and the process tapers off.

When the diffusion curve reaches its maximum, diffusion has reached its *prevalence level*. When prevalence reaches everyone, or almost everyone, the prevalence level has reached saturation. *Saturation,*

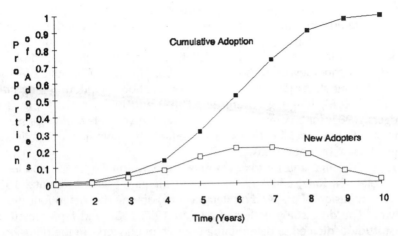

Figure 1.1. Typical cumulative adoption S-shaped curve for the diffusion of innovations

Note. The S-shaped diffusion curve indicates that early in the diffusion process few people adopt the innovation, but over time more individuals adopt until all (or almost all) members of the system adopt the innovation. Data are from Ryan and Gross (1943) and represent the cumulative proportion of adopters of hybrid corn seed among farmers in two Iowa communities.

then, is the maximum number of adopters reached when an innovation has completely diffused. Generally, saturation is considered to occur at 100%, but sometimes diffusion only reaches 70% or 80% (or even less) of the population and, in such cases, saturation is not achieved. For example, in the United States, telephones are owned by about 90% of the population, but in some developing countries telephone ownership hovers around 50% or 60%. Thus, the prevalence of telephones in the United States is high and almost at saturation, whereas the prevalence of telephones in other countries is low and not near saturation. The datasets reanalyzed in this book vary from low prevalence to saturation.

Ryan and Gross did not study the exact patterns of who-to-whom network influences in the diffusion process, and hence did not collect network data (Burt & Minor, 1983; Boissevain, 1974; Knoke & Kuklinski, 1982; Scott, 1991; Wellman, 1983). Network models of diffusion split off from the mainstream of rural sociological research on the diffusion of innovations and represent a subset of the diffusion paradigm.

Diffusion of innovations theory has been applied extensively to how farmers decide to adopt farm innovations. In the diffusion paradigm, farmers are classified as early or later adopters depending on their time of adoption. Numerous variables have been shown to be related to innovativeness as measured by time of adoption including education, income, cosmopoliteness, contact with change agents, and many more (Rogers, 1983).

Diffusion of innovations theory has also been applied to the diffusion of family planning practices (Rogers & Kincaid, 1981), diffusion of educational innovations (Carlson, 1964; Rogers 1983), the spread of new medical technology (Anderson & Jay, 1985; Greer, 1977), policy innovations among states (Walker, 1969), fluoridization adoption among cities (Crain, 1966), language (Renfrew, 1989) and many more topics (see Rogers, 1983, for a comprehensive review). However, few of these studies investigate how social networks and the flow of communication influence the diffusion of innovations.

The first and best-known network diffusion study was conducted by Coleman, Katz, and Menzel (1966; Coleman, Menzel, & Katz, 1957) on the diffusion of a new drug (tetracycline) among doctors in four Illinois towns. The drug study collected data in 1955-1956 and represented the first study dedicated to determining the role of networks in the diffusion of an innovation. Briefly, the results (discussed in more detail below) indicated that diffusion occurred more quickly among integrated doctors than among socially isolated doctors and that different networks were influential at different times during diffusion.

At about the same time, Rogers and Beal (1958) collected data on time of adoption of various farm innovations and network data on who farmers communicated with regarding farm practices. They found that interpersonal communication among farmers was important in convincing farmers to try and adopt farm practices.

These two studies established a research tradition of network models of diffusion. The history of network models can be traced from Coleman, Katz, and Menzel's (1966; Menzel & Katz, 1955) and Rogers's (1962; Rogers, Ascroft, & Röling, 1970) opinion leadership to Granovetter's (1973, 1982) strength-of-weak-ties, to Rogers and Kincaid's (1981) communication networks and finally to Burt's (1987) structural equivalence model. The field of network diffusion models can be divided into two types: (a) relational models, and (b) structural models (Burt, 1987; Rice, 1993).

Relational and structural network diffusion models are presented in Chapters 3 and 4, respectively. *Relational network* diffusion occurs when interpersonal influence flows through direct ties. The classic model of opinion leadership is considered a relational model. *Structural network diffusion* occurs when interpersonal influence is a function of an individual's position in his or her social structure.

Diffusion network models of social change have an inherent advantage over most collective behavior models because diffusion network models study the exact pattern of who-to-whom relations. In collective behavior (and many other) models, individuals are assumed to have complete knowledge of the behavior of everyone in the social system. In contrast, network models allow the specification of whom and to what degree individuals monitor others in the social system, based on the system's social structure. Thus, network models capture the structure of communication and incorporate this structure into predictions of individual behavior.

DIFFUSION VERSUS COLLECTIVE BEHAVIOR

Diffusion and collective behavior models are applied to a wide range of social change processes from crossing the street to adopting complex technological innovations. Collective behavior examples include such processes as riots, revolutions, and community action which are often political in nature. In contrast, other examples of collective behavior such as choosing a seat at a restaurant, walking across the street, or deciding to leave a boring lecture come from everyday life. These social behavior examples are different from diffusion of innovations examples which are equally ubiquitous, yet should be understood in a different light.

In the diffusion of innovations, adoption decisions often entail some risk[1] or decision making under uncertainty. For example, a farmer who decides to plant a new strain of seed in his or her farm has incomplete information about how much yield the new seed will provide. As such, the farmer is taking a risk by buying the new seed and deciding to plant the seed without having complete information about how the seed will perform. Farmers who adopt early have more uncertainty than farmers who adopt the seed later. The presence of risk and uncertainty during the diffusion of an innovation means that individuals are more likely to rely on the behavior of immediate others rather than on some perception as to what the social norm is. That is, risk and uncertainty force individuals to turn to their peers to gain more information and/or reassurance about potential adoption decisions.

In collective behavior, individuals may more easily rely on some vague perception of normative behavior. In other words, in collective behavior risk is usually considerably lower because the consequences of engaging in the behavior are considerably less. Collective behavior does not usually demand an outlay of money, for example. Collective behavior is also characterized by rather certain outcomes. The probabilities for two courses of action are rather better known for collective behavior. Conversely, in the diffusion of innovations, the outcomes to adoption are

---

[1]Risk and uncertainty, particularly in the diffusion of innovations, are often used interchangeably. Although their effects are usually similar, they are different concepts. *Risk* is the amount of a potential resource lost, whereas *uncertainty* is the degree that outcomes are unknown (also see Cancian, 1979).

considerably more uncertain, particularly for early adopters because they do not have the experience of prior adopters from which to learn.

Thus, it is likely that networks play a larger role in structuring the rate and character of diffusion of innovations than collective action. These network models provide a window through which to see threshold and critical mass effects in diffusion, and then by analogy to collective behavior. To analyze thresholds and the critical mass in the context of diffusion network models, this book reanalyzes three classic diffusion datasets.

DATASETS ANALYZED

Few studies have been conducted on network models of diffusion. Conducting a study to collect both time-of-adoption and network data as well as other covariates is extremely difficult, yet at least five studies have done so (Table 1.1). Of the five best-known diffusion network studies, three have data that exist in the public domain, whereas two can no longer be analyzed because the data are lost.

Table 1.1. Six Diffusion Studies that Collected Network and Time-of-Adoption Data.

	Authors	Title	Year Data Collected	Data Available?
1.	Beal and Rogers (1958)	Collins Study	1955	No
2.	Coleman, Katz, and Menzel (1966)	Drug Study	1955	Yes
3.	Rogers (1964)	Colombian Farmers	1962	Yes*
4.	Becker (1970)	Public Health Officials	1969	No
5.	Rogers, Ascroft, and Röling (1970)	Three Country Study	1966-1969	Yes
6.	Rogers and Kincaid (1981)	Korean Family Planning	1973	Yes

*The specific network nominations are not available, only the sum of nominations received.

The three studies with time-of-adoption and network data used in this book are:

1. Medical Innovation—4 communities, 125 respondents
2. Korean Family Planning—25 communities, 1,047 respondents
3. Brazilian Farmers—11 communities, 692 respondents.

Table 1.2 reports the relevant characteristics of these three datasets. The total time of adoption for the three studies ranges from 18 months to 20 years, the percent of cumulative adoption, prevalence, ranges from 29% to 98% thus providing data from both high- and low-adoption communities. A majority of the data were collected in non-U.S. settings and represent technological change processes. In contrast, the medical innovation study was conducted with doctors in four Illinois communities.

Table 1.2. Data Reanalyzed in this Book.

	Medical Innovation	Brazilian Farmers	Korean Family Planning
Country	USA	Brazil	Korea
Number of Respondents	125 Doctors	692 Farmers	1,047 Women
Number of Communities	4	11	25
Innovation	Tetracycline	Hybrid corn	Family planning
Length of Time for Diffusion	18 months	20 years	11 years
Year Data Collected	1955	1966	1973
Average Time of 50 % Adoption	6	16	7
Highest Prevalence	89%	98%	83%
Lowest Prevalence	81%	29%	44%
Citation	Coleman et al. (1966)	Rogers et al. (1970)	Rogers & Kincaid (1981)

Nonlinear regression (Valente, 1993) was conducted on the three datasets to measure the rate of diffusion with the following logistic function:

$$y^{(t)} = \frac{Ne^{Nat}}{(N-1 + e^{Nat})}$$

where y(t) is the cumulative proportion of adopters, N is the population size, a is the rate of diffusion, and t is the time period. The symbol e is the base of the natural logarithm which is approximately 2.72. Speed of diffusion rate parameters were computed for each community in the three datasets and are reported in Appendix C.

Medical Innovation

Coleman, Katz, and Menzel of Columbia University's Bureau of Applied Research studied the adoption of tetracycline by physicians[2] in four Illinois communities in 1954. Katz had circulated a proposal to study the process of interpersonal influences on behavior change. This proposal was an extension of research that he conducted earlier on the role of the mass media and interpersonal influence in voting, fashion, and consumer decisions (Katz, 1957; Katz & Lazarsfeld, 1955). One of the Bureau's alumni was director of market research for Charles Pfizer and Company, a large pharmaceutical firm located in New York.

Pfizer was interested in determining how physicians decide to adopt a new drug so that it could more effectively market its products through salesmen and promotional media. Pfizer provided a grant of $40,000 to the Bureau's researchers to apply Katz's proposal to study the diffusion of tetracycline, introduced in 1953. A pilot test was conducted in a New England community to test the research instruments (Menzel, 1960). The main study was conducted in early 1955 in four Illinois communities: Peoria, Bloomington, Quincy, and Galesburg.

Tetracycline was a powerful and useful antibiotic just introduced in the mid-1950s. Pfizer hoped tetracycline would diffuse rapidly because it was a tremendous improvement over existing antibiotics. Pfizer could then use the lessons learned from the tetracycline study for the marketing of other drugs.

The drug study contained two important methodological advances over previous diffusion studies: (a) the collection of a behavioral measure of time of adoption by inspecting the prescription records in the pharmacies in the four Illinois communities, and (b) network analysis. The drug study inspected the prescription records of the pharmacies in the four

---

[2]Caplow and Raymond (1954) conducted probably the first medical sociology diffusion study, although it did not affect later studies in this tradition.

communities to determine when the 125 physicians actually adopted the innovation. This objective measure of time of adoption represented an important improvement over prior diffusion studies, which relied on the respondent's recall of their time of adoption.[3]

Although the methodological improvement of examining prescription records was a substantial step forward, the data collected on time of adoption were still biased. The researchers could not examine all of the prescription records in all pharmacies for the one-and-a-half year period of study. Instead, the researchers inspected the prescription records on three consecutive days each 28 days. Consequently, some doctors may have prescribed tetracycline on a day not captured in the 3-day sampling scheme and thus been assigned a later adoption date than their actual adoption date. The exact degree and type of bias is unknown.

A second shortcoming of the sampling technique was that the researchers were measuring first trial, not necessarily adoption (Rogers, 1962). First trial is the first use of an innovation. For example, first trial of tetracycline was the first time a doctor prescribed the drug to a patient. Adoption is the continued use of an innovation. Adopters may have only prescribed tetracycline to a small proportion of their patients and only gradually included the drug in their repertoire of existing therapies. Thus, the adoption process may or may not have continued.

Social network data were collected by asking doctors in the four communities to name three doctors whom they most frequently sought for discussion, friendship, and advice. These three questions enabled doctors to list the names of three other doctors with whom they discussed medical practices, and then three other doctors from whom they sought advice with regard to medicine. Finally, they were asked to name three other doctors who were considered friends.

The three networks elicited from these questions provided a picture of the social structures of the four medical communities. Doctors varied on how many doctors they named who lived in their own community. That is, some doctors named physicians from other towns or states not covered in the study. Also, doctors varied on degree of similarity or difference in the three networks. That is, some doctors named the same three doctors for discussion, friendship and advice, whereas others named three different doctors each time.

In the study, five personal characteristics (in addition to network characteristics) were found to influence a physician's decision to adopt

---

[3]The study showed that doctors consistently estimated that they adopted the innovation earlier than was discovered in the prescription records, although this discrepancy may have been due to the manner in which the prescription records were sampled, which consisted of inspecting prescription records on three consecutive days every 28 days.

tetracycline: belief in science, professional age, number of journals subscribed to, prescription-prone medical practice, and detail-man contact (Burt, 1987). In other words, science oriented, younger, prescription-prone doctors and those who subscribed to more journals and met with a sales representative from the drug company were more likely to be earlier adopters of tetracycline.

Brazilian Farmers

In the mid-1960s, Rogers and others conducted an ambitious "three country study" to determine influences on adoption of farm practices in Nigeria, India and Brazil (Herzog, Stanfield, Whiting, & Svenning, 1968; Rogers, Ascroft, & Röling, 1970; Rogers & Shoemaker, 1971). The "three country study" was conducted in three phases. The first phase determined existing agricultural practices and trained agricultural extension workers. The second phase, which is the one of interest here, was designed to survey farmers in these villages using standard survey techniques and network analysis to determine influences on adoption. The third phase was a follow-up to determine how well the innovation diffused. Network data were collected by asking farmers to name their three best friends, the three most influential people in their community, the three most influential people regarding various farm innovations, and the best person to organize a cooperative project.

Only in Brazil, and only for hybrid corn, did adoption of the innovation reach more than a small proportion of the farmers. This book reanalyzes the data from the Brazilian farmers study using the network measures and time of adoption of hybrid corn. In addition, variables found to correlate with time of adoption and of interest to the present theory were: (a) cosmopoliteness as measured by visits to the nearest large city and contact with family members living elsewhere, and (b) contact with external sources of information such as the mass media and agricultural extension agents.

Korean Family Planning

Scholars at Seoul National University's School of Public Health (Park, Chung, Han, & Lee, 1974) collected data on the adoption of family planning methods among all married women of child-bearing age in 25 Korean villages in 1973 ($N = 1,047$). Network data were obtained by asking respondents to name five people from whom they sought advice about family planning, general information, abortion, health, the purchase of consumer goods, and children's education. Adoption data were obtained by asking respondents to state the year they first used a modern family planning method. In this dataset, external contact was measured with a media campaign exposure scale reproduced in Appendix C (Dozier, 1977; Lee, 1977; Rogers & Kincaid, 1981).

These three datasets have some limitations in their study designs: namely, two of them (Brazilian farmers and Korean family planning) rely on recall for measuring time of adoption which may not be a reliable measure (Coughenour, 1965; see also Nischan, Ebeling, Thomas, & Hirsch, 1993, for studies that show accuracy of recall data). Also, they represent rural populations in developing countries whose behavior may be quite different from urban individuals in the 1990s or beyond. However, these data represent the only data available for studying network models of diffusion. Analysis of this data provides information and results to understand the diffusion of innovations process.

These three datasets constitute 40 communities with a fairly broad array of diffusion process. That is, the rate of adoption is not uniform across studies. For example, diffusion of tetracycline among the doctors occurred rather rapidly and in such a manner that indicates little interpersonal interaction was necessary for the diffusion of this new drug. In contrast, diffusion of hybrid seed corn occurred slowly, and hence adoption of hybrid corn in Brazil may have been more a function of interpersonal influence rather than mass media influence or strong personal predispositions.

Figure 1.2 presents diffusion curves for 12 of the 40 communities under study here. Notice that the curves for the four medical innovation communities rise steeply from the early time periods. In fact, after only six months, over half of the doctors adopted tetracycline. In contrast, for the Korean family planning and Brazilian farmers studies, diffusion occurred much more slowly. Brazilian farmers took 16 years, and Korean women took 7 years for half of the respondents to adopt the innovation.

This indicates that personal preferences or some outside force such as a media or sales campaign were active in facilitating tetracycline's diffusion. For the Brazilian farmers and Korean women, diffusion was influenced by word of mouth or interpersonal communication/persuasion. Thus, contagion was more likely a factor in the spread of hybrid corn and family planning than in the spread of tetracycline. This book clarifies the role of contagion and explicitly models the contagion process in the diffusion of innovations.

CONTAGION

Contagion refers to the specific process of innovation diffusion. For example, when we refer to a disease as contagious we mean that the disease spreads through person-to-person contact. If a fad is contagious, then we imply that individuals will take up a fad if they see someone else doing it.

In the diffusion of innovations, *contagion* refers to how individuals monitor others and imitate their behavior to adopt or not adopt innovations.

The Diffusion Effect

Rogers (1983) refers to contagion as the *diffusion effect*. "The diffusion effect is the cumulatively increasing degree of influence upon an individual to adopt or reject an innovation, resulting from the activation of peer networks about an innovation in a social system" (Rogers, 1983, p. 234). Thus, individuals are exposed to the innovation through their network of peers, and this exposure has a cumulatively increasing influence on adoption behavior as pressure toward conformity builds.

The network methods and models presented in the ensuing chapters explore the diffusion effect by modeling how the cumulative influence on interpersonal networks affects diffusion of innovations. The diffusion effect provides the justification for modeling network exposure influences on adoption in a cumulative manner. That is, we assume that once an individual has adopted the innovation they remain adopters and do not

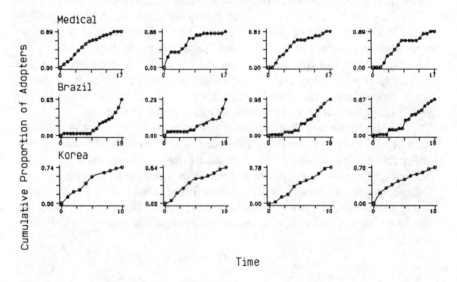

Figure 1.2. Diffusion curves for 12 of the 40 communities

Note. Notice that the curves are shaped very differently. The medical innovation diffusion curves (top row) accelerate quickly, thus reaching a high proportion of adopters early. The Brazilian farmers' curves have a long growth period before a high proportion of adopters is reached. The Korean family planning diffusion curves represent the in-between case; some early acceleration, but still a relatively long lag phase.

discontinue their adoption or develop negative attitudes toward the innovation, thus resulting in negative role models.

To be sure, many adopters never adopt, discontinue adoption, or spread negative information about an innovation (Barnett, Fink, & Debus, 1989). *Nonadoption* is the nontrial of an innovation, and *discontinuance* is the rejection of an innovation after it has previously been adopted (Rogers, 1983, p. 21). Nonadoption is most likely in the case of Korean family planning in which some women may have suffered side effects from a family planning practice or spread negative information about it. But, in general, most adopters probably continued adopting and provided positive information about the innovation.

The diffusion effect is most often modeled with mathematical models of diffusion in which adopters influence non-adopters at a specified rate (Hamblin, Jacobsen, & Miller, 1973; Monin, Benayoun, & Sert, 1976). Table 1.3 shows a hypothetical diffusion case of 100 potential adopters in which adopters influence nonadopters to adopt at a 1% rate. With five initial adopters, 4.75 additional adopters are recruited ($4.75 = 5 \times 95 \times .01$) for Time Period 2. Now at Time Period 3 there are 9.75 adopters and 90.25 nonadopters who interact, and 1% of those interactions result in adoptions: 8.8 new adopters. Thus, after Time Period 3 there are 18.55 adopters (9.75 + 8.8). This diffusion effect continues until everyone in the system has adopted, which yields the diffusion curve shown in Figure 1.3.

It is generally assumed that contagion of an innovation occurs when individuals model the behavior of near-peers. Individuals are likely

Table 1.3. Hypothetical Diffusion When Adopters Influence Nonadopters at One Percent.

	Cumulative Adopters:	Cumulative Nonadopters:	Rate:	New Adopters: axbxc	Cumulative Adopters: a+d
Time	a	b	c	d	e
1	0	100	.01	0	0
2	5	95	.01	4.75	9.75
3	9.75	90.25	.01	8.8	18.55
4	18.55	81.45	.01	15.11	33.66
5	33.66	66.34	.01	22.33	55.99
6	55.99	44.01	.01	24.64	80.63
7	80.63	19.37	.01	15.62	96.25
8	96.25	3.75	.01	3.61	99.86
9	99.86	.14	.01	.14	100
10	100				

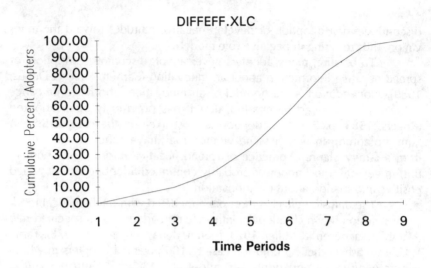

Figure 1.3. Hypothetical diffusion curve based on adopters persuading nonadopters at a rate of 1% in a sample of 100 individuals with five initial adopters

to imitate adoption behavior if they witness that behavior among others who are similar to themselves, or even of a slightly higher status. Contagion by modeling the behavior of those with whom we are in direct contact is referred to as contagion by cohesion.

Burt (1987) has argued that contagion is more likely to occur through structural equivalence (structural equivalence is covered in Chapter 5). Contagion via structural equivalence is the imitation of the behavior of others who are in a similar position in the social space, but not necessarily others with whom the potential adopter communicates. Thus, contagion via structural equivalence may be a more exact specification of modeling the behavior of near-peers because near peers are those with whom one is equivalent.[4]

Contagion is central to the thesis of this book because contagion is the social process of how individuals form opinions and eventually adopt or not adopt an innovation. Contagion, then, is the lens through which individuals monitor the behavior of others, and it leads to influences in adoption behavior. Contagion can occur via cohesion (direct ties), structural equivalence (social proximity), popularity (centrality), or it can be system wide (using system adoption level as the measure). These four contagion

---

[4]The duality of cohesion and structural equivalence appears in the literature on interpersonal communication, which argues that women may be more concerned with cohesive ties and men more responsive to structurally equivalent ones (Gray, 1993; Tannen, 1993).

processes define those other individuals in the social system who influence an individual's behavior. In addition to who in the social system is an influence, individuals also vary in the degree of others' influence.

The degree of contagion influence represents the second dimension of contagion. For example, contagion via cohesion can occur for direct ties, but may also occur for indirect ties. Contagion from indirect ties expands an individual's lens of perception to include more people in his or her realm of influence. In later chapters we discuss both the who and degree of contagion influence for various network models. Figure 1.4 shows the relevant dimensions of contagion.

Contagion is the interpersonal influence process that operates both via direct ties and status comparison, and it operates via immediate and more distant others. But the effect of contagion is not necessarily linear, that is, its influence is not constant across individuals and across time. Rather, the effect of contagion occurs in distinct tipping points called thresholds for individuals and the critical mass for systems. Threshold and critical mass effects represent an exciting new development in diffusion theory.

	Direct ties	Status Comparison
Close	Immediate nominations	SE matrix raised to high power (e.g., $v = 16$)
	Ties of ties	SE matrix raised to lesser power (e.g., $v = 8$)
	Ties of ties	SE matrix raised to lesser power (e.g., $v = 4$)
Far	Flow matrix	SE matrix

Figure 1.4. Contagion occurs along two dimensions: cohesion, represented by direct ties, and status comparison, represented by similarity of position, and near versus far others

Prior Research on Threshold and Critical Mass Effects*

The majority of recent diffusion network research has been on threshold and critical mass models used to explain the rate of adoption of an innovation, collective behavior, or the rise and fall of public opinion (Granovetter, 1978; Marwell, Oliver, & Prahl, 1988; Schelling 1978). Threshold and/or critical mass effects have been postulated to operate in a wide variety of contexts, ranging from riots to the spread of political revolutions. Scholars argue that certain conditions lead to a critical mass or that the existence of a certain threshold leads to some type of behavior or outcome (Neuman, 1990).

Threshold models of collective behavior postulate that an individual engages in a behavior based on the proportion of people in the social system already engaged in the behavior (Granovetter, 1978). An individual's adoption of collective behavior is thus a function of the behavior of others in the group or system. Individuals with low thresholds engage in collective behavior before many others do, whereas individuals with high thresholds do so only after most of the group has engaged in the collective behavior.

An individual's *threshold* is the proportion of a group needed to engage in a behavior before the individual is willing to do so. For example, an individual threshold for joining a riot is the proportion of rioters an individual must see rioting before he or she is willing to join (Granovetter,

*Special thanks to Everett M. Rogers for help with this chapter.

1978). An individual with a low threshold adopts a behavior when few others have, whereas an individual with a high threshold adopts only after many others have. The distribution of thresholds is postulated as one cause for the variance in rates of adoption. Threshold models, explored in Chapter 4, show that the threshold concept can be quite complex.

The *critical mass* is thought to occur early in the diffusion process when about 10% to 20% of the population has adopted an innovation. The critical mass occurs here because it is believed that this is the number of individuals needed to spread the innovation to the rest of the social system. As noted in Figure 1.1 earlier, the critical mass for hybrid seed corn diffusion is thought to have occurred at about 1935 for that data. Once the critical mass is reached, diffusion of the innovation accelerates until adopters outnumber nonadopters, after which time the diffusion process slows (discussed in detail in Chapter 5). This simple treatment of the critical mass has many caveats and many pitfalls.

Before the detailed analysis of threshold and critical mass models, however, this chapter presents a review of prior research and theories on these models. Threshold and critical mass effects occur in a wide range of areas. The breadth of applications, as is shown in the remainder of this chapter, attests to the wide applicability of threshold and critical mass models. The field of studies reviewed present different means to measure an individual's influence network and show how similar approaches have emerged in a wide variety of contexts.

EPIDEMIOLOGY

In epidemiology, Kermack and McKendrick (1927) provided the first systematic treatment of the threshold concept by showing that the occurrence of an epidemic is partly determined by population density. If the infectivity rate (the transmission rate or its contagiousness) of a disease is the same for two populations with different densities, the population with a density above a given threshold level experiences an epidemic, whereas a population with a density below the threshold level does not (Bailey, 1957/1975; Black, 1966; Kermack & McKendrick, 1927).

Whittle (1955) expanded and formalized this work in a stochastic threshold theorem that stated that the probability of an epidemic depends on: (a) the size of the population, and (b) the ratio of the average time that it takes for a pair of individuals to communicate (density) and the average time that an infector is virulent (transmission effectiveness). Epidemiologists use this threshold theorem to determine the probability that an epidemic will occur, given values for density and contagion.

However, epidemiologists make assumptions about contagion that prohibit their models from being directly applicable to social behavior. For example, an epidemic has the same virulence regardless of the specific individuals involved in transmission, but in social contagion, the effectiveness of one person in persuading another individual to change depends on the persuader's perceived characteristics, such as credibility, expertise, trustworthiness, and so on.

In genetics, Boorman and Levitt (1980) created a network model of the spread of genetic traits through a population. The Boorman and Levitt model argues that genes gain prominence in a gene pool once they reach a certain threshold of existence. In fact, the genes may stay dormant and not manifest themselves for many generations until they pass the threshold, then flourish in the population. Other researchers (Cavalli-Sforza, 1991) have conducted similar modeling in computer simulations and the analysis of cultural traits.

GEOGRAPHY

The diffusion of diseases, such as cholera (Pyle, 1969), has received attention in the geography literature because diseases spread through space. In fact, geographers have made considerable contributions to our understanding of the diffusion of innovations by recognizing that the environment channels the paths for diffusion (Brown, 1981). In other words, certain environmental or topological factors control the pathways of diffusion and thus, to some extent, determine when an individual may adopt.

Geographers have debated two complementary theories for the diffusion of innovations: spatial distance, and urban hierarchy (Brown, 1981; Casetti, 1969; Casetti & Semple, 1969; Huang & Gould, 1974; Hudson, 1969; King, 1984; Morrill, Gaile, & Thrall, 1988). The spatial distance theory argues that innovations diffuse radially out from a point of origin. Locations close to the origin adopt earlier, whereas locations further away adopt later. The urban hierarchy model of diffusion argues that innovations generally originate in the largest city, diffuse next to cities of the next class in size, then to smaller cities, and then to still smaller cities, and so on. The urban hierarchy model adds structure to the diffusion process by including city population size.

These two theories of diffusion create a duality of the diffusion process between direct contact and structural simularity. That is, adopting units may adopt innovations by imitating others with whom they have direct contact, or may adopt by imitating others to whom they are equal. There are numerous reasons why either of these processes may occur for a given innovation. The important point is that geographers specified the direct contact versus structural equivalence debate in terms of physical distance for direct contact and urban population size for hierarchical equivalence. The duality is explored in considerable detail in Chapters 3, 4, and 7.

Hägerstrand (1967) pioneered geographical research on the diffusion of innovations in his 1953 dissertation on the diffusion of Swedish farm practices. Hägerstrand developed a model of diffusion that consisted of adopters embedded in a "mean information field" (MIF), a set of information and influence probabilities determined by the individual's location in the community. An individual's MIF was a set of probabilities that indicated the likelihood that he or she would communicate with individuals who lived in other geographic areas. The contact probabilities represented measures of influence, and individuals were hypothesized to adopt innovations when this influence surpassed the individual's resistance.

The geography literature recognized the importance of threshold levels in diffusion and generally equated the term threshold with resistance (Brown, Malecki, Gross, Shrestha, & Semple, 1974; Hägerstrand, 1967; Morrill, Gaile, & Thrall, 1987). But the term threshold was more often used to determine or denote adopter characteristics that prohibited or promoted adoption. For example, Pederson (1970) created city population thresholds that determined whether cities were able to adopt an innovation. However, Ray, Villeneuve, and Roberge (1974, p. 341) stated that thresholds can be measured as to the minimum size of the adopting unit and the number of times a potential adopter has to be contacted before adopting. This second component is consistent with the model developed later in this book.

Geographical methods translated spatial distances into contact probability networks and analyzed diffusion within these networks (Haggett, 1976). The debate between spatial and hierarchical models yielded to an understanding that both processes were valid explanations for diffusion. Eventually it was seen that spatial and hierarchical models could be combined into a general model in which each position marked the end of an extreme. That is, a general model could be created that contained a parameter for spatial and one for hierarchical effects (Casetti & Semple, 1969; Pederson, 1970, p. 219). In sum, geographers recognized the importance of thresholds and provided a spatial analog to the cohesion versus structural equivalence duality.

MARKETS AND ECONOMIES

Rohlfs (1974) argued that the interdependence of consumers alters traditional supply/demand economics. Interdependence is a situation in which an individual's behavior affects the corresponding behavior of other individuals in a system. *Interdependence* drives threshold and critical mass models because it is the interdependence of the actors in a system that adds value to an innovation for its adopters and thus leads to adoption or rejection.

For example, if a consumer purchases a particular computer software package, the purchase increases the consumer base for that program, thus lowering its price and increasing the level of social and technical support available for the product. An individual's purchase, and that of millions of other consumers, gradually increases the incentive for others to buy the product. Interdependence for an innovation is often communicated directly as persuasion messages through personal networks.

Interdependence is most obvious in the provision of interactive media such as the telephone, electronic mail, or fax (Markus, 1987). If one person owns a telephone, it is of little utility. However when two people own telephones, its utility increases slightly. As more people buy telephones, the marginal utility of owning a telephone increases yet again for each individual adopter. Notice that the benefits of the innovation increase with each additional adoption for future adopters and for all past adopters (a point which we discuss shortly).

Arthur (1989, 1990) argued that as competing technologies compete for market share, chance events may allow one technology to gain an initial market advantage. With technologies that enjoy increasing returns to scale (such as the telephone), the initial technology enjoys an advantage that makes it more likely to gain market dominance.

Interdependence of consumers in a market may lead to inferior technology (David, 1985). Inferior technologies can occur when a particular manifestation of a technology gains a foothold in the market. As the diffusion process progresses, the initial manifestation of the technology becomes the standard, and change from this initial standard is difficult. For example, David (1985) showed that the initial keyboard layout designed for the typewriter (the QWERTY keyboard) was constructed to slow down typing speed because early typewriters had keys that jammed if one typed too quickly. However, the QWERTY technology is clearly inferior and not appropriate for computers because one can "key" as quickly as finger speed allows. The presence of interdependence and increasing returns to scale make it difficult to change from the obsolete keyboard layout to more efficient designs (such as the Dvorak keyboard).

Interdependence is necessary for threshold effects to occur. If there is no interdependence among adopters, then thresholds remain constant during the diffusion process. It is the interdependence of adopters that raises or lowers individual thresholds. Once an individual adopts an innovation, it lowers the risk of adoption to all other individuals; they therefore lower their thresholds due to the decreased risk. Without interdependence, the change in risk of adoption to others is not communicated, which may occur through lower prices, more sales and service outlets, and so on.

For example, the first person to use a spreadsheet in an office may do so because he or she used it in a prior office or due to a sales campaign or due to contact with another user. Once this first individual adopts this spreadsheet in the organization he or she lowers the risk for others to adopt it because they now have someone to turn to as an example and to gain support. Thus, other individuals in the organization may lower their threshold for adopting the spreadsheet program. Individual reductions in thresholds have an aggregate effect by accelerating the rate of adoption, thus resulting in an earlier critical mass.

Network externalities are forces outside the buyer-seller exchange relationship that affect the outcome of the exchange. Examples of network externalities are government regulations, the availability of an adequate infrastructure, and, most importantly, the number of existing adopters/purchasers of the innovation. Network externalities may be direct in nature, such as the increased marginal utility of an additional adopter in the telephone example mentioned earlier. Network externalities can also be indirect, as in the case of the additional availability of compatible computer software, or for phones, the availability of phone lines, service outlets, and answering machines. Finally, network externalities can arise due to an expanded service network for consumers. Network externalities are a sign that the supply and demand relationship between producer and consumer does not fully explain the outcome of a buyer-seller exchange. Thus, market share has a strong influence on continued product success (Katz & Shapiro, 1986).

Network externalities have been used to develop pricing strategies for interactive media. Oren and Smith (1981) discussed the economics of a pricing strategy for a telecommunications network provider such as a telephone company. Their analysis showed that network providers should offer the network service at a lower price to early users (thus providing a high incentive to adopt). Early users then provide an incentive for later users to adopt, which is referred to as *sequential interdependence*. In sum, markets are strongly influenced by the interdependence of consumers, which in turn makes markets vulnerable to threshold effects.

COLLECTIVE BEHAVIOR

Sociologists at the University of Wisconsin (Marwell, Oliver, & Prahl, 1988; Oliver & Marwell, 1988; Oliver, Marwell, & Teixeira, 1985; Prahl, Marwell, & Oliver, 1991; also see Olson, 1965) studied the critical mass in collective behavior. This research describes variables that affect the critical mass such as network characteristics and interest and resource heterogeneity, as well as the role of free riders, selective incentives, and group membership.

Free riders (individuals who benefit from a collective action without contributing to it), selective incentives, and other variables may alter the critical mass. Free riders delay the critical mass because they do not contribute to the collective action and provide disincentives for those who do. *Selective incentives*, rewards for participating in a collective action, may cause the critical mass to occur earlier. Incentives create motivation for some individuals to join a collective action, which in turn creates the perception that joining the collective action is a popular activity. The greater participation makes it easier to achieve a critical mass. Resources, of course, may also influence collective action critical mass. If an individual with considerable resources donates to a collective action, then the critical mass is more likely to be achieved.

Oliver and Marwell conducted their research mainly with computer simulations that do not address thresholds explicitly. However, they argued that free riders have higher thresholds of participation and hence do not contribute to the provision of the public good until its provision is assured. The critical mass is determined by characteristics of the members of a social system such as the presence of free riders, selective incentives, variable resources, and group membership.

Other collective action theorists (Macy, 1990) have taken a learning curve perspective. Macy's argument is that collective action systems reach a stable state, but that the presence of learning in the system may accelerate the critical mass.

INTERACTIVE COMMUNICATION TECHNOLOGIES

Markus (1987, 1990) posited the existence of *reciprocal interdependence*, the interdependence of later adopters on earlier adopters, and vice versa. Sequential interdependence occurs when earlier adopters make decisions that affect later adopters. Reciprocal interdependence exists when later adopters of an innovation provide benefits to earlier adopters by reciprocating their communication. Reciprocal interdependence helps diffuse a telecommunications service (or some other innovation) and tends to prevent existing adopters from discontinuing.

For example, early users of fax machines were frustrated by their inability to send faxes to many other individuals or businesses. However, as more people and organizations purchased fax machines, they provided a greater incentive for earlier adopters to use the fax. Thus, later adopters provided reciprocal interdependence to earlier adopters. Consequently, Markus suggests that critical mass effects are stronger for innovations that benefit from universal access[1] such as the telephone, electronic mail, and the fax.

Reciprocal interdependence rarely affects thresholds because users or consumers have already made an adoption decision. That is, once

---

[1]*Universal access* is the ability to reach all members of a community through a communication medium (Markus, 1987).

an individual has adopted, his or her threshold has been met. Reciprocal interdependence occurs after an individual has adopted because reciprocal interdependence is the influence of later adopters on earlier adopters. However, reciprocal interdependence does insure that the critical mass does not slip away by insuring that those individuals who have already adopted an innovative medium do not discontinue using it.

In sum, interactive communication technologies are a special case of market forces with higher levels of interdependence among actors. The greater interdependence (both sequential and reciprocal) results in increased threshold and critical mass influences.

PUBLIC OPINION

Bandwagon research attempts to determine whether individuals are influenced by the proportion of individuals in a system who support or oppose an issue or candidate (Ceci & Kain, 1982; Lang & Lang, 1984). Little support for direct bandwagon effects has been found in prior research, but Navazio (1977) found that poll results had differential effects for different occupational categories. Bandwagons are the public opinion version of thresholds which argues that there is a level of public support for an opinion that triggers other individuals to support such an opinion. Research is needed on the determinants of bandwagon thresholds.

Krassa (1988) posited that groups, networks, and opinion leadership drastically alter the public opinion framework. Krassa conducted computer simulations to demonstrate how the differential importance that individuals place on the opinions of others affects the rate at which public opinion changes due to a contagion process. In other words, opinion leadership[2] affects thresholds and the critical mass. Krassa asserted that the more integrated a community, the more quickly a dominant public opinion becomes widespread and the easier it is for a few opinion leaders to affect this outcome.

More generally, threshold and critical mass models provide insight into mass media communication. Early research conducted on the effects of the media on public opinion asserted that the media influence people in a two-step flow[3] (Katz, 1957; Katz & Lazarsfeld, 1955). That is, the media disseminate information to opinion leaders who then influence opinion followers. Public opinion formation is a process in which individuals develop

---

[2]*Opinion leaders* are individuals who influence other individuals' attitudes or behavior informally in a desired way with relative frequency (Rogers, 1983, p. 27).

[3]The *two-step flow* of communication model posits that the media influence individuals' opinions in two steps by first disseminating information which is then mediated by interpersonal networks (Katz, 1957; Katz & Lazarsfeld, 1955).

opinions through their interaction with networks of family and friends[4].

The *spiral of silence* theory (Noelle-Neumann, 1977, 1984) states that the perceived distribution of public opinion concerning an issue determines an individual's decision to express his or her opinion. For example, individuals may support efforts to recycle plastic and glass bottles, yet keep these opinions to themselves until they perceive enough public support to feel safe in expressing this opinion. More exact models of social influence may permit the testing of the spiral of silence theory and help researchers determine threshold levels of spiral of silence effects (Price & Allen, 1990).

Pluralistic ignorance occurs when a minority opinion on a subject is incorrectly perceived as a majority opinion (O'Gorman & Garry, 1976). The concepts of the spiral of silence and pluralistic ignorance do not discuss critical mass models per se, yet they are both related to a critical mass effect (Taylor, 1982). Neuman (1990) postulated a threshold response for public opinion and agenda setting. That is, the relationship between the media's coverage of an issue (the media agenda) and the public's attentiveness to that issue (the public agenda) is not a linear, but rather a logistic function. This indicates that both threshold and critical mass effects occur in the agenda-setting process.[5]

Often, individuals adopt certain opinions when their threshold for that opinion is reached. Once a critical mass of individuals with a certain opinion is reached, the spread of that opinion then accelerates. One strategy is to communicate an opinion to a few influential people who make up a core critical mass. These opinion leaders then disseminate the information to the populace. As the proportion of people adopting that opinion increases, the thresholds of nonadopters decrease.

For example, public support for recycling efforts to preserve the environment is increased when popular personalities make public appearances in support of recycling. The promotions by these opinion leaders lower the thresholds of the public. As thresholds to recycling are met, more people adopt recycling, thus convincing others in their personal network to adopt as well. At some point, a critical mass of recyclers is reached that insures continued recycling and widespread adoption.

The dynamics of critical mass models led Kuran (1987, 1989) to formulate a theory of "collective conservatism" that states that individuals

---

[4]A second area of mass media effects that may be influenced by threshold and critical mass effects is that of mass media consumption. Seasonality in television viewing behavior (Barnett, Chang, Fink, & Richards, 1991) is highly normative. That is, individuals develop patterns of media consumption that become habitualized and therefore subject to social pressure.

[5]Agenda setting is the process in which the mass media set the agenda for the public by influencing the salience of attitudes toward an issue (McCombs & Shaw, 1972).

falsify their political preferences as long as they feel threatened. However, once an individual perceives that there are enough people in a social system who support his or her political preference, he or she no longer suppresses his or her true political beliefs. Kuran shows how the theory explains the French, Russian, and Iranian revolutions. In sum, bandwagons, opinion spirals, pluralistic ignorance, revolutions, and media effects are influenced by threshold and critical mass levels.

DECAY PROCESSES

So far, we have discussed threshold and critical mass effects for processes that are expected to have widespread adoption. However, threshold and critical mass processes may also apply to *decay processes*, situations in which members of a social system discontinue adoption, defect from a collective action, or leave an organization. In these applications, a system does not continuously decay, but rather starts to decay slowly, then the decay accelerates until some critical point after which the decay is almost impossible to stop.

For example, Panko (1988) found that different levels of electronic mail use can cause electronic mail systems to fail. That is, some members may rarely use the electronic mail system, and their nonuse inclines others to use the system less frequently because their messages are not reciprocated. This process reinforces itself and results in a system in which total use declines.

White flight models explain racial shifts in urban neighborhoods (Schelling, 1978). White flight models argue that some residents leave a neighborhood if it starts to become integrated. As a few residents leave, the proportion of integration increases slightly, thus inclining a few more residents to leave. A critical level is reached at which flight from the neighborhood is difficult to stop, and then the neighborhood becomes completely populated by the new racial group.

Another decay process is job turnover or defections from an organization. Krackhardt & Porter (1986; see also Hirschman, 1972) demonstrated that turnover in an organization is often a function of interpersonal communication relationships rather than a random process. In other words, an individual tends to quit his or her job when others with whom they communicate quit a job. Consequently, organizations can experience a situation in which a few members leave, which induces their communication partners to leave, which induces still more people to leave, and so on. In the extreme, there comes a critical point when the organization fails due to the loss in membership and expertise.

SUBGROUPS

The critical mass effect may operate at the subgroup level. That is, when the critical mass is reached among a subgroup of a population, it provides incentives for members of the subgroup to adopt the innovation. Prior research (Rice, Grant, Schmitz, & Torobin, 1990) demonstrated that threshold effects are more likely to occur among members of the same group. That is, people in the same workgroup are more likely to have similar thresholds and thus similar times of adoption of an interactive innovation such as an electronic messaging system.

Allen (1988) showed that subgroups may have different critical mass points. As the result of research on the rate of adoption of the French Minitel[6] system, Allen concluded that the critical mass was reached for certain videotex services before it was reached for other services. That is, the critical mass may be reached for one subgroup of a system before it is reached for other subgroups or the whole system. In subsequent research, Allen (1990) argued that a new shopping mall seeks to first sign up a few "anchor" stores, large retailers that put a mall "on the map," which then attracts other stores to lease space in the mall. In this way, more certainty is established for the investors who build the mall, and they have insurance the mall will succeed.

Often it is the percentage of relevant others that adopt an innovation that determines the threshold level influence for an individual, not the absolute number or percentage in the social system. Thus, in an organization, if enough members of an individual's workgroup or division use an electronic mail system, critical mass has been reached for that subgroup, regardless of the behavior of the rest of the individuals in the organization (Rice, 1990).

CONCLUSION

This chapter has provided a common framework to understand threshold and critical mass models. The framework consists of a diffusion paradigm in which individual tipping points of action are thresholds and the group tipping point is the critical mass. Seven sets[7] of research provide some general conclusions regarding threshold and critical mass effects. The conclusions are:

---

[6]French Minitel is a videotex service that is provided throughout France by the French public telecommunication agency used for teleshopping, a telephone directory service, and as an electronic messaging system.

[7]Research on decision-making processes that also use threshold models was omitted because decision making does not involve interdependent individuals and is thus not amenable to network models (Beach, Hope, Townes, & Campbell, 1982; Shorrett, 1983).

- Thresholds are influenced by both direct contact and the hierarchical equivalence of adopters and nonadopters.
- Markets are composed of interdependent consumers who are influenced by threshold and critical mass effects (even so far as to result in inferior technology standards).
- Social attributes of the members contributing to a collective action affect the critical mass.
- Interactive communication technologies have higher interdependence and thus stronger threshold and critical mass effects.
- Threshold and critical mass effects influence public opinion and accentuate pluralistic ignorance and opinion or revolution spirals.
- Threshold and critical mass effects also occur for decay processes resulting in declines in interactive technology use, racial segregation, and organizational failure.
- Threshold and critical mass effects may also occur in subgroups.

These fields of research show that different factors control the network of communication, that impacts when individuals adopt innovations. Every field has contained an implicit or explicit theory of thresholds to adoption, and each field has contributed something to our understanding of how communication networks are formed and act as sources of persuasion. In this sense, each of these areas of research can be tied to a specific operationalization of the general threshold model.

Table 2.1 summarizes the literature described in this chapter and specifies the mechanism by which the activity of other adopters in the system is communicated to a focal individual. The activity thus represents an influence on adoption coming from another individual in the system. Each of of these influences, then, can be translated into the network (matrix weighting) models presented in the following chapters.

Greater understanding of many diffusion processes can be

Table 2.1. Literature Reviewed and the Mechanisms by Which Network Influences are Communicated Between Adopters and Nonadopters.

Field of study	Mechanism for network influence
Geography	Spatial location
Markets and economics	Consumer behavior
Collective action	Interest and resources
Public opinion	Attitude
Interactive communication technology	New channels of communication
Subgroups	Determine the domain of potential communication partners

gleaned from a general model of diffusion using threshold and critical mass effects. The existence of threshold and critical mass points indicates that two situations that seem almost identical can result in completely different behaviors both at the individual and group level. It helps explain why riots occur in some settings, yet do not occur in seemingly identical settings. It also helps explain why some products diffuse to everyone, yet other products that seem just as advantageous diffuse to no one.

However, no one has presented a unified framework within which to analyze diffusion and collective behavior in threshold or critical mass terms. The network approach advocated in this book provides such a framework.

═Relational Diffusion═ Networks

This chapter reviews and presents research conducted on relational diffusion networks. *Relational diffusion networks* posit that direct contacts between individuals influence the spread of an innovation. Four types of relational models are discussed: (a) opinion leadership, (b) group membership, (c) personal and network density, and (d) personal network exposure. These four relational models posit that an individual's direct contacts influence his or her decision to adopt or not adopt an innovation.

A *network* is the pattern of friendship, advice, communication, or support that exists among members of a social system (Burt & Minor, 1983; Knoke & Kuklinski, 1982; Scott, 1991; Wellman, 1983). Networks may be constructed by asking respondents to name others with whom they communicate. Once these nominations are made, a graph of the communication structure can be drawn that indicates who communicates with whom.[1] This graph is called a *sociogram*. Figure 3.1 presents an example of a sociogram for one community of the Korean family planning study discussed earlier (Rogers & Kincaid, 1981).

The graph depicts the direct ties between women in one village for the family planning network. Each circle represents one woman with her

---

[1]Networks may also be constructed by observing who talks with whom, or of collecting data through archival records such as marriage records, electronic mail communication, examination of diaries, and so on. Bernard and Killworth (with Sailer, 1982; Killworth, Bernard, & McCarty, 1984) questioned the validity of nomination techniques of data collection (see Marsden, 1990, for discussion).

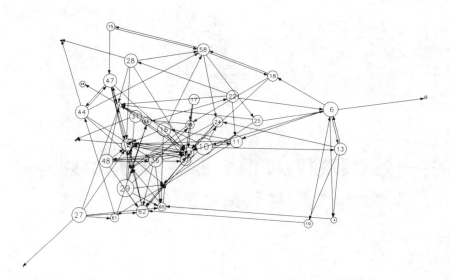

Figure 3.1. Sociogram of who-to-whom contacts for Korean family planning village 24 from the matrix of contacts in Table 3.1

Note: Each circle represents an individual (the identification numbers from the study are written inside) and the width of the circle is proportionate to the number of nominations received. The arrows represent unidirectional nominations and the positions of individuals are drawn such that those receiving the most nominations are located near the center.

respondent ID in the center of the circle. The lines connecting women represent woman-to-woman communication. Each line has a direction indicated by the arrows such that an arrow pointing from one person to another indicates that that person nominated the other. For example, person #10 nominated person #13, and #13 did not reciprocate that nomination.

The pattern of communication can be converted to a matrix of who-to-whom ties in which the rows refer to which individuals send communication and the columns refer to which individuals receive the communication. The matrix in Table 3.1 is the who-to-whom matrix that created the sociogram in Figure 3.1. The matrix can then be read into computer programs such as UCINET, STRUCTURE, GRADAP, NEGOPY, or SNAPS for network analysis computations.

The initial network approach to diffusion research was to count the number of times an individual was nominated as a network partner and correlate this value with innovativeness as measured by time of adoption (Becker 1970; Coleman, Katz, & Menzel 1966; Rogers, 1962; Rogers

& Kincaid, 1981). The number-of-nominations score yielded a rough measure of how integrated an individual was in the network, which provided a measure of opinion leadership.

OPINION LEADERSHIP

The first and most powerful network model was the use of nominations to determine who in the social system is considered an opinion leader. *Opinion leaders* were defined as those individuals with the highest num-

Table 3.1. Matrix of Who-to-whom Nominations for the Korean Family Planning Village Number 24 Which Indicates Which Individuals Communicate with Which Others.

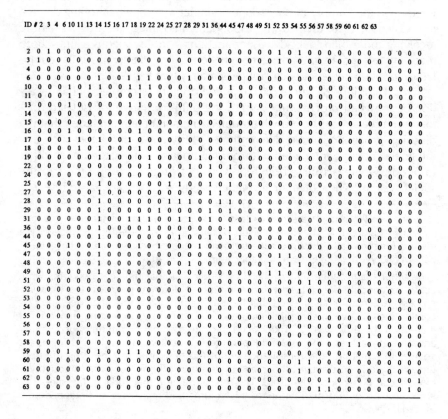

ID #	2	3	4	6	10	11	13	14	15	16	17	18	19	22	24	25	27	28	29	31	36	44	45	47	48	49	51	52	53	54	55	56	57	58	59	60	61	62	63
2	0	1	0	0	0	0	0	0	0	0	0	0	0	0	0	0	0	0	0	0	0	0	0	1	0	1	0	0	0	0	0	0	0	0	0	0	0	0	0
3	1	0	0	0	0	0	0	0	0	0	0	0	0	0	0	0	0	0	0	0	0	0	1	0	0	0	0	0	0	0	0	0	0	0	0	0	0	0	0
4	0	0	0	0	0	0	0	0	0	0	0	0	0	0	0	0	0	0	0	0	0	0	0	0	0	0	0	0	0	0	0	0	0	0	0	0	0	0	1
6	0	0	0	0	0	0	1	0	0	1	1	1	0	0	0	1	0	0	0	0	0	0	0	0	0	0	0	0	0	0	0	0	0	0	0	0	0	0	0
10	0	0	0	1	0	1	1	0	0	1	1	1	0	0	0	0	0	1	0	0	0	0	0	0	0	0	0	0	0	0	0	0	0	0	0	0	0	0	0
11	0	0	0	1	1	0	1	0	0	0	1	0	0	0	1	0	0	0	0	0	0	0	0	0	0	0	0	0	0	0	0	0	0	0	0	0	0	0	0
13	0	0	0	1	0	0	0	0	0	1	1	0	0	0	0	0	0	0	1	0	1	0	0	0	0	0	0	0	0	0	0	0	0	0	0	0	0	0	0
14	0	0	0	0	0	0	0	0	0	0	0	0	0	0	0	0	0	0	0	0	0	0	0	0	0	0	0	0	0	0	0	0	0	0	0	0	0	0	0
15	0	0	0	0	0	0	0	0	0	0	0	0	0	0	0	0	0	0	0	0	0	0	0	0	0	0	0	0	0	1	0	0	0	0	0	0	0	0	0
16	0	0	0	1	0	0	0	0	0	1	0	0	0	0	0	0	0	0	0	0	0	0	0	0	0	0	0	0	0	0	0	0	0	0	0	0	0	0	0
17	0	0	0	1	1	0	1	0	0	1	0	0	0	0	0	0	0	0	0	0	0	0	0	0	0	0	0	0	0	0	0	0	0	0	0	0	0	0	0
18	0	0	0	0	1	0	1	0	0	1	0	0	0	0	0	0	0	0	0	0	0	0	0	0	0	0	0	0	0	0	0	0	0	0	0	0	0	0	0
19	0	0	0	0	1	1	0	0	0	0	1	0	0	0	1	0	0	0	0	0	0	0	0	0	0	0	0	0	0	0	0	0	0	0	0	0	0	0	0
22	0	0	0	0	0	0	0	0	0	0	1	0	0	0	1	0	1	0	1	0	0	0	0	0	0	0	0	0	0	1	0	0	0	0	0	0	0	0	0
24	0	0	0	0	0	0	0	0	0	0	0	0	0	0	0	0	0	0	0	0	0	0	0	0	0	0	0	0	0	0	0	0	0	0	0	0	0	0	0
25	0	0	0	0	0	1	0	0	0	0	0	0	1	1	0	0	1	0	1	0	0	0	0	0	0	0	0	0	0	0	0	0	0	0	0	0	0	0	0
27	0	0	0	0	0	0	1	0	0	0	0	0	0	0	0	0	1	1	0	0	0	0	0	0	0	0	0	0	0	0	0	0	0	0	0	0	0	0	0
28	0	0	0	0	0	1	0	0	0	0	0	1	1	1	0	0	1	1	0	0	0	0	0	0	0	0	0	0	0	0	0	0	0	0	0	0	0	0	0
29	0	0	0	0	0	1	0	0	0	0	0	1	0	0	0	0	1	0	1	0	0	0	0	0	0	0	0	0	0	0	0	0	0	0	0	0	0	0	0
31	0	0	0	0	0	0	1	0	0	1	1	1	0	0	1	1	0	1	0	0	0	1	0	0	0	0	0	0	0	0	0	0	0	0	0	0	0	0	0
36	0	0	0	0	0	0	1	0	0	0	0	0	1	0	0	0	0	0	0	1	0	0	0	0	0	0	0	0	0	0	0	0	0	0	0	0	0	0	0
44	0	0	0	0	0	1	0	0	0	0	0	0	1	0	0	1	0	1	1	0	0	0	0	0	0	0	0	0	0	0	0	0	0	0	0	0	0	0	0
45	0	0	1	0	0	1	0	0	1	0	0	1	0	1	0	0	1	0	0	0	0	0	0	0	0	0	0	0	0	0	0	0	0	0	0	0	0	0	0
47	0	0	0	0	0	0	1	0	0	0	0	0	0	0	0	0	0	0	0	0	0	0	0	1	1	0	0	0	0	0	0	0	0	0	0	0	0	0	0
48	0	0	0	0	0	0	1	0	0	0	0	0	0	1	0	0	0	0	1	0	0	1	0	1	1	0	0	0	0	0	0	0	0	0	0	0	0	0	0
49	0	0	0	0	0	0	1	0	0	0	0	0	0	0	0	0	0	0	0	1	1	1	0	0	0	0	0	0	0	0	0	0	0	0	0	0	0	0	0
51	0	0	0	0	0	0	0	0	0	0	0	0	0	0	0	0	0	0	0	0	0	0	0	0	1	0	0	0	0	0	0	0	0	0	0	0	0	0	0
52	0	0	0	0	0	0	0	0	0	0	0	0	0	0	0	0	0	0	0	0	0	0	0	0	1	0	0	0	0	0	0	0	0	0	0	0	0	0	0
53	0	0	0	0	0	0	0	0	0	0	0	0	0	0	0	0	0	0	0	0	0	0	0	0	0	0	0	0	0	0	0	0	0	0	0	0	0	0	0
54	0	0	0	0	0	0	0	0	0	0	0	0	0	0	0	0	0	0	0	0	0	0	0	0	0	0	0	0	0	0	0	0	0	0	0	0	0	0	0
55	0	0	0	0	0	0	0	0	0	0	0	0	0	0	0	0	0	0	0	0	0	0	0	0	0	0	0	0	0	0	0	0	0	0	0	0	0	0	0
56	0	0	0	0	0	0	0	0	0	0	0	0	0	0	0	0	0	0	0	0	0	0	0	0	0	0	0	0	0	0	0	1	0	0	0	0	0	0	0
57	0	0	0	0	0	0	1	0	0	0	0	0	0	0	0	0	0	0	0	0	0	0	0	0	0	0	0	0	0	1	0	0	0	0	0	0	0	0	0
58	0	0	0	0	0	0	0	0	0	0	0	0	0	0	0	0	0	0	0	0	0	0	0	0	0	0	0	1	1	0	0	0	0	0	0	0	0	0	0
59	0	0	0	1	0	0	1	0	0	1	1	0	0	0	0	0	0	0	0	0	0	0	0	0	0	0	0	0	0	0	0	0	0	0	0	0	0	0	0
60	0	0	0	0	0	0	0	0	0	0	0	0	0	0	0	0	0	0	0	0	0	0	0	0	1	1	0	0	0	0	0	0	0	0	0	0	0	0	0
61	0	0	0	0	0	0	0	0	0	0	0	0	0	0	0	0	0	0	0	0	0	0	0	0	1	1	0	0	0	0	0	0	0	0	0	0	0	0	0
62	0	0	0	0	0	0	0	0	0	0	0	0	0	0	0	0	0	1	0	0	0	0	0	0	0	0	0	1	0	0	0	0	0	0	0	0	0	0	1
63	0	0	0	0	0	0	0	0	0	0	0	0	0	0	0	0	0	0	0	0	0	0	0	0	0	1	1	0	0	0	0	0	0	0	0	0	1	0	0

ber of nominations and were theorized to be a significant influence on the rate of adoption. Once identified, opinion leaders were discovered to be earlier adopters of innovations, and it was postulated that opinion leaders then passed on information to opinion followers. This pattern of opinion leaders being early adopters and then passing on information about the innovation to opinion followers is called *the two-step flow hypothesis* (Katz, 1957; Robinson, 1976; Weimann, 1982). A model of the two-step flow hypothesis is presented in Figure 3.2.

Generally, individuals wait until the most influential members of the group adopt an innovation. After the opinion leaders adopt, risk and uncertainty about the innovation decrease and opinion followers are more likely to adopt the innovation. This two-step flow hypothesis is useful for explaining the spread of public opinion, fashions, new technologies, and so forth. The two-step flow hypothesis was tested in the medical innovation study by Coleman, Katz, and Menzel (1966).

Coleman et al. (1966) stated that for integrated doctors, those who were well-connected in the network, diffusion occurred as a chain reaction process in which adopters influenced nonadopters, resulting in a steady increase in the number of new adopters similar to a snowball rolling down a hill. Coleman et al. divided the respondents into integrated doctors—those receiving more than four advice nominations—and isolated doctors—those receiving fewer than four advice nominations. They then graphed the cumulative adoption curve for each group separately (see Figure 3.3).

The diffusion curve for integrated doctors resembles a chain-reaction or snowball process. In contrast, the diffusion curve for isolated doctors resembles a logistic growth model.[2] Coleman et al. concluded that the diffusion process occurred differently for the two sets of doctors such that integrated doctors interacted with one another and persuaded each other to adopt, whereas isolated doctors were not influenced by others in the social system.[3] The Coleman and others study was very similar to research

---

[2]Logistic growth models are curves that follow an S-shaped pattern like the one shown in Figure 1.1. They are logistic because they can be approximated by a logistic function, and they are called growth models because that is the general pattern observed in the growth of plants, animals, and so forth.

[3]The other main conclusion of the drug study was that different networks were active as conduits for diffusion and adoption at different stages in the diffusion process. Coleman et al. showed that the professional networks of advice and discussion were active in spreading the new drug early in its diffusion. They argued that when the drug was first introduced into the medical community, uncertainty about its efficacy and the risk of adoption forced doctors to turn to their peers for advice, information, and reassurance about the new drug. As the drug diffused, uncertainty and perceived risk decreased, and thus diffusion occurred through the more social network of friendship. The role of different networks in the spread of innovations is not pursued further in this volume and represents an untapped area of study.

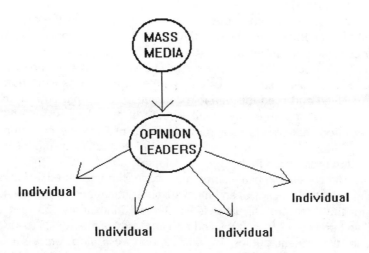

Figure 3.2. Two-step flow hypothesis of media influence

Note: The mass media influence opinion leaders who in turn influence other individuals.

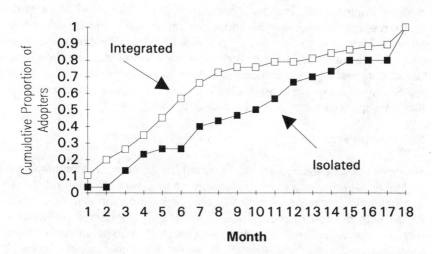

Figure 3.3. Diffusion curves for integrated versus isolated doctors in the medical innovation study (Coleman, Katz, & Menzel, 1966)

conducted on the diffusion of farm innovations (Katz, 1962; Katz, Levine, & Hamilton, 1963).

At about the same time Coleman et al. collected the drug study data in Illinois, Rogers and Beal (1958) collected similar data on adoption of agricultural innovations by farmers in Collins, IA, and shortly thereafter Rogers (1962) collected similar data in five villages in Colombia, South America. The Colombia study calculated the number of network nominations received and used this variable as a measure of opinion leadership. Innovativeness, measured by recall of time of adoption, was correlated with opinion leadership, especially in more progressive communities (Rogers, 1962). Is there support for the opinion leadership model in the three datasets analyzed in the present volume?

The correlation between opinion leadership (measured as the number of nominations received) and innovativeness (measured by time of adoption) for the three present datasets is: Medical innovation, .23 ($p < .01$); Brazilian farmers, .17 ($p < .001$); and Korean family planning, .25 ($p < .001$). Thus, for the present studies, *we find support for a moderate association between opinion leadership, measured by the number of nominations received, and innovativeness, measured by time of adoption.* From this data it is not possible to say whether early adoption influences opinion leadership or vice versa. In other words, causality is still open to question, but clearly there is an association between opinion leadership and early adoption.

One may argue that individuals who receive a lot of nominations are more influential and act as role models for others. As such, they scan their environment for new ideas, opinions, and products, and adopt earlier. Conversely, individuals who adopt innovations early may be viewed by others as more progressive and be perceived as desirable communication partners. As such they tend to receive more nominations. Furthermore, because individuals tend to nominate those of higher socioeconomic status (SES) and higher SES is associated with earlier adoption, the correlation may be a spurious effect of this confounding variable.[4]

Nominations Sent

Although not a measure of opinion leadership, the number of nominations an individual sends is a crude measure of connectedness for an individual in a network. This measure indicates how active a person is in communication with the rest of the social system. Highly connected individuals receive information and influence concerning an innovation earlier than less connected individuals. Therefore, we expect connectedness, as measured by nominations, sent to be correlated with innovativeness. The cor-

---

[4]A second area of debate with regard to opinion leadership is whether individuals act as opinion leaders on one (monomorphic) or many (polymorphic) different products or opinions (Merton, 1968; Rogers, 1983).

relation between connectedness and innovativeness is: Medical innovation, .13 (p = NS); Brazilian farmers, .01 (p = NS); Korean family planning, .15 ($p < .001$). Thus, connectedness, as measured by network nominations sent, is not associated with early adoption, with the exception of the Korean family planning study.[5]

The correlation results of these studies and other research establishes empirical evidence for a diffusion network model as follows: Opinion leaders, measured by the number of nominations received, adopt innovations relatively early, and then, based on communication with these opinion leaders, other individuals imitate their behavior and adopt later. However, other diffusion studies showed that marginal individuals were more likely to be earlier adopters of innovations. Menzel (1960), one of the co-authors of the medical innovation study, argued that marginal individuals are free from social norms and thus able to be earlier adopters of innovations. Indeed, because innovations are new (by definition) they are often perceived as conflicting or contrary to existing conventions, thus they are difficult for integrated individuals to adopt. To resolve this conflicting evidence regarding the role of marginal individuals and perceived normativeness of innovations, Becker (1970) conducted a study among public health officials.

Becker's Study of High- and Low-Adoption Potential Innovations

Becker surveyed 103 public health officials in Michigan, Illinois, and New York with regard to network and time-of-adoption data for two health innovations: diabetes screening and measles immunization. Becker wanted to know whether opinion leaders always adopted innovations earlier, or whether opinion leaders adopted innovations earlier only when the innovation was obviously advantageous.

Diabetes screening had low adoption potential (LAP) and was unlikely to diffuse rapidly, whereas measles immunization had high adoption potential (HAP) and was expected to diffuse rapidly. Becker's research results showed that more advantageous innovations (HAP) are likely to be adopted earlier by central figures in the network or those receiving many network nominations. In contrast, risky innovations (LAP) were more likely to be adopted earliest by marginal members of the network, that is, those receiving the fewest network nominations.[6]

---

[5]The positive association between connectedness and innovativeness for the Korean data is probably due to the fact that the Korean family planning campaign prompted adopters of family planning to communicate with others in their villages and thus act as proponents for the innovation.

[6]Stern, Craig, La Greca, and Salem (1976) replicated Becker's study and showed that central faculty members in a university were the first to adopt a computer information system.

In sum, opinion leaders are identified by the number of network nominations they receive,[7] and they adopt innovations relatively earlier if these innovations are consistent with the system's norms and if the innovation has high adoption potential. This was the case in the studies of doctors' adoption of tetracycline and farmers' adoption of hybrid corn. However, if the system's norms do not favor adoption or if the innovation has low adoption potential (entails considerable risk or uncertainty), then opinion leaders may delay their adoption.

The opinion leader framework remains one of the most useful and parsimonious network models available. Yet Becker's research showed that the perceived advantageousness of the innovation was an important component of the diffusion process. Two subcultures may perceive an innovation differently, so that it is considered advantageous in one system, whereas another group may consider the same innovation disadvantageous.

Furthermore, there may be a different value placed on adoption of innovations. In some groups (or cultures) adopting new ideas is a sign of modernity which is highly valued, whereas for other groups or cultures new ideas are considered deviant and more value is placed on tradition. These group norms have a strong influence on adoption behavior. Indeed, as Becker's (1970) research showed, group norms are important determinants of adoption behavior. Thus, another relational network diffusion model was posited in which individuals adopt innovations based on the behavior of the group to which they belong.

GROUP MEMBERSHIP

Individuals who are connected to one another in a group are more likely to share information with one another and hence reach common understandings and perceptions when faced with a new product or idea. Consequently, individuals in the same group can be expected to have similar adoption times. This is particularly true for innovations that are highly interdependent such as electronic communication (Rice, Grant, Schmitz, & Torobin, 1990).

As mentioned in Chapter 2, *interdependence* is the degree an individual's adoption behavior is dependent on others' adoption. For telephones, electronic mail, and faxes, an individual's adoption behavior depends on having others who have adopted in order to have someone with whom to communicate. Group membership increases the social pressure on an individual to adopt an innovation in order for the whole group to share in the benefits. For example, if an individual belongs to a workgroup that has

---

[7]This is essentially a crude measure of network centrality which is discussed in more detail in the next chapter.

decided to use an electronic mail system to communicate, he or she will receive strong social pressure to use the system or else quit the group.

There are a variety of ways to define group membership in network analysis (see Scott, 1991, pp. 103-125). A typical approach is that an individual is a member of a group if 50% or more of his or her communication is with others in that group. Another common practice is to define any set of three or more individuals as a group if their communication density is greater than the communication density for the network (Richards, 1989).

The trouble with these group definitions is that they cannot uniquely partition the network because an individual may be a member of numerous groups in the network. Consequently, in our attempt to determine if group membership results in similar adoption times, we cannot use a group definition that results in any one member belonging to more than one group. Therefore, we chose to examine the components of the network.

A *component* is a set of points that are linked to one another (Scott, 1991, p. 105). Two individuals are members of the same component if they can reach one another through any series of intermediaries. The three datasets (medical innovation, Brazilian farmers, and Korean women) can be broken down into components and analyzed to determine if group membership is a significant influence on adoption of innovations. The three datasets comprise 40 communities, and each community is symmetrized on reciprocity[8] and divided into components.

The degree of similarity of adoption times was measured by conducting analysis of variance to determine if the average adoption time between components was greater than that within components. In other words, if group membership affects adoption, individuals in the same component should adopt an innovation at about the same time. The results show that group membership, as defined by component membership, was not associated with innovation adoption. Individuals in the same component were not necessarily more likely to adopt innovations at about the same time than individuals in other components (see Appendix C).

In 11 of the 40 communities, individuals in the same group had significantly different adoption times than individuals in another group. It should be noted that in all 11 communities in which adoption times did differ significantly between groups, the largest component had an earlier adoption time. That is, the difference was found to occur when a group existed that adopted the innovation later than the majority in the social system.[9]

---

[8]To symmetrize on reciprocity means to change the network such that only when two individuals nominate each other is there considered a link between them. Symmetrizing on reciprocity yields more sparse networks.

[9]In this analysis isolates were removed from the networks because prior research found that isolates were more likely to be later adopters of innovations (Rogers & Kincaid, 1981).

Isolates

Isolates are individuals who are not connected to anyone else. Isolates should be later adopters of innovations because they are less likely to become aware of innovations through interpersonal channels of communication. Moreover, isolates are less likely to hear about prior positive experiences that earlier adopters can share. Finally, isolates are less likely to receive social support in their adoption decisions. Are isolates later adopters of innovations in the present datasets?

The reanalysis of the three datasets showed that isolates were more likely to be later adopters of innovations. For the medical innovation data, the average time of adoption for isolates was after 9.5 months compared to 7.9 months for the rest of the sample (p = ns). Brazilian farmer isolates adopted at 16.6 years compared to nonisolates who adopted after 14.7 years ($p < .05$). Korean women isolates adopted an average of 1.6 years later than their nonisolate counterparts ($p < .05$). Network isolation, then, does yield considerably later adoption times.

The opinion leader model provides evidence that individuals most prominent in the system, those receiving many nominations, are earlier adopters of innovations. The group membership model indicates that in some systems individuals tend to adopt innovations when others in their group adopt the innovation, but this is not a generalized phenomenon. At the extreme case of network isolation, isolates were found to be later adopters. These two relational models, opinion leadership and group membership, examine who nominates whom in the network and predict adoption behavior based on that information. A third means to conceive of relational network influence during diffusion is to determine whether an individual's personal network reaches out to the network or whether it is constrained to itself.

PERSONAL NETWORK DENSITY

Personal network density is the degree an individual's personal network is interconnected. A dense personal network is composed of numerous connections between the people one nominates as communication partners. Dense personal networks are also referred to as integrated, interlocking, or tight-knit. In a dense personal network, an individual's communication partners also communicate frequently with one another.

An individual with a dense network is not likely to receive much information from outside his or her own restricted set of communication partners (Danowski, 1986). Thus, individuals with dense networks are more likely to hear of an innovation later and are thus, on average, later adopters of innovations. Figure 3.4 shows a dense (interconnected) and a radial personal network.

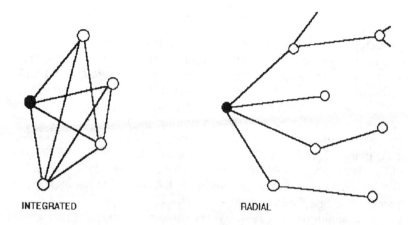

INTEGRATED   RADIAL

Figure 3.4. A dense and a radial interpersonal network

Density scores for the personal networks of the 1,864 individuals in the studies were computed by dividing the number of nominations between network partners by the number of interpersonal network nominations possible (Scott, 1991, pp. 74-76). The correlation between personal network density and innovativeness, as measured by time of adoption for the three studies is: medical innovation, .01 (p = ns); Brazilian farmers, .03 (p = ns); and Korean family planning, .16 ($p < .001$). The absence of correlation indicates that density is not associated with earlier or later adoption. In other words, individuals who have personal networks that are interconnected do not adopt innovations later. It is interesting to note that a weak correlation between density and time of adoption exists in the Korean family planning network. This is not surprising because the adoption of family planning often requires considerable social support that would be more forthcoming in dense personal networks.

Nondense networks are radial and indicate that an individual nominates others who do not necessarily know or talk to one another. As Figure 3.4 shows, the individual with a radial personal network has contacts to people who do not nominate one another. *Radial personal networks* are characterized by communication outside the focal individual's personal network. Individuals with radial networks receive more information through their network because it reaches beyond the set of their immediate communication partners. Radiality, then, is an important relational property that enables an individual to hear about and thus adopt an innovation early. Personal network radiality is measured with the Guimarães (1972) relative integration index:

$$Radiality = \frac{[(Max(Geod) + 1 - (Geod)]_{i+}}{n - 1}$$

in which Geod is the geodesic matrix (distance), and the portion in brackets is its inverse (i.e., closeness). The numerator is then summed, and n is the size of the network. This formula provides a measure for each individual that indicates how close he or she is to all others in the network.

The correlation between personal network radiality and innovativeness as measured by time of adoption for the three studies is: medical innovation, .26 ($p < .01$); Brazilian farmers, .14 ($p < .001$); and Korean family planning, .18 ($p < .001$). These significant correlations indicate that radiality is associated with early adoption. In other words, individuals who have personal networks that extend out to the rest of the network are more likely to adopt innovations earlier.

In addition to the personal network density/radiality measures, the network as a whole has a density measure. *Network density* is the degree of connectedness in a network and is measured by the ratio of existing links to the total number possible:

$$Density = \frac{T}{n(n - 1)/2}$$

in which T is the number of ties and n is the number of individuals in the network.[10] As personal network density is associated with later adoption, *network* density is associated with faster diffusion.

High network density indicates that there is a lot of communication among individuals in the network. The more frequent communication facilitates information and influence flow through the network, thus representing, on average, a greater likelihood that individuals in the network will hear about the innovation earlier and be persuaded to adopt earlier. The correlation between network density and rate of diffusion for the three studies is:[11] medical innovation, .97 ($p < .05$); Brazilian farmers, .61 ($p < .05$); and Korean family planning, .49 ($p < .05$). Thus, these correlations suggest that community connectedness facilitates faster innovation spread.

Network density does not, however, lead to more extensive diffusion. That is, more dense networks are not more likely to have innovations

---

[10]This is the density equation for symmetric networks (any relation between two individuals is reciprocated; see Richards, 1989, for a discussion of symmetry and reciprocity). The density equation for an asymmetric network is:

$$Density = \frac{T}{n(n-1)}$$

[11]These correlations should be interpreted with some caution because the number of cases for each dataset is the number of communities and therefore represents small samples: medical innovation, $n = 4$; Brazilian farmers, $n = 11$; Korean women, $n = 25$.

spread to a greater proportion of the network. The correlation between network density and proportion of the network who eventually adopt an innovation is:[12] medical innovation, -.17 (p = ns); Brazilian farmers, -.12 (p = ns); and Korean family planning, .25 (p = ns). These numbers, although interpreted with caution, indicate that connectedness is not associated with spread of the innovation. The higher network density leads to some restriction of the innovation from all members of the community. Again notice that for family planning the direction of association is different; higher network density leads to a more extensive spread.

The density measure provides one means of examining how an individual's personal network influences his or her adoption behavior. Another means to determine how an individual's network determines his or her adoption behavior is through personal network exposure.

PERSONAL NETWORK EXPOSURE

Personal network exposure is the degree an individual is exposed to an innovation through his or her personal network. Individual influence is the amount of exposure that an individual receives through patterns of interaction in the network. Individual influence models argue that individuals make decisions based on information they receive from those to whom they are exposed (Rice, 1993). Often, it is a person's connectedness in a social system that influences his or her adoption behavior. Connectedness is the number of others in a social system that to whom an individual is linked by some relation. *Connectedness* measures how much exposure to an innovation an individual receives. If an individual is connected to many others who have adopted an innovation, his or her exposure is high. This exposure may or may not result in adoption, depending on an individual's threshold (reviewed in Chapter 5).

Figure 3.5 provides a personal network exposure example for one doctor of the medical innovation data in which every doctor had a personal network from 0 to 9 other doctors (Coleman, Katz, & Menzel, 1966). Figure 3.5a shows a typical personal network for a doctor (from Peoria, identification number three) connected to five people: two friends, two discussion partners, and one advice partner. Figure 3.5b shows the same personal network three months later by which time two of his or her discussion partners had adopted. Now the individual is exposed to the innovation by his or her personal network, and the degree of exposure is directly computed from the personal network by dividing the number of adopters, 2, by the size of the personal network, 5. Thus, exposure equals 40% for this doctor at time period three.

---

[12]Again, these correlations represent extremely small samples.

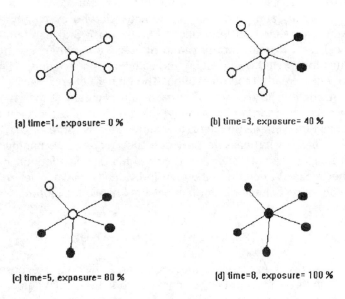

(a) time=1, exposure= 0 %   (b) time=3, exposure= 40 %

(c) time=5, exposure= 80 %   (d) time=8, exposure= 100 %

Figure 3.5. Personal network exposure to an innovation for a medical doctor (data are from Coleman, Katz, & Menzel, 1966)

Note: Time Period One is shown in 1 (a) above when there are no adopters. In 1 (b), two discussion partners adopted and so exposure is 2/5 or 40%. In 1 (c) the two friendship partners adopted by Time Period Five and so exposure is 4/5 or 80%. Finally, in 1 (d) all of the individual's personal network partners adopted, so exposure is 100%. The threshold is the individual's exposure at time of adoption.

As this doctor's direct ties adopt tetracycline, they expose him or her to the innovation through their direct communication. As the innovation diffuses, personal exposure increases because more individuals adopt, until every individual has exposure of 100%. Personal network exposure is a measure of the direct influence on an individual to adopt an innovation.

In addition to this direct influence, network exposure surrounds an individual with adopters, thus instilling the belief that adoption is the norm for the individual. Regardless of the behavior of the social system as a whole, the individual is surrounded with others who have adopted the innovation. Thus, his or her network of peers, as defined by direct ties, has accepted the innovation.

Furthermore, these direct ties are contributing to network externalities (see Chapter 2) and other effects that increase the persuasive influence of adoption. For example, if an individual is surrounded by direct ties who have adopted family planning, he or she has more information on possible side effects, where to get advice, additional supplies, and so on. Thus, the individual's network of peers facilitates his or her adoption by prematurely reducing risk and uncertainty about the innovation.[13]

The geodesic is used to include the nomination of nominees. The *geodesic* is the number of steps on the shortest path between any two points (Harary, Norman, & Cartwright, 1965). If two individuals have a geodesic of one they are directly connected, they nominate one another. If two individuals have a geodesic of two, then they are indirectly connected through one intermediary (two steps). In other words, a geodesic of two implies that two individuals—John and Paul—know one another only through Mary. A geodesic of three indicates that three steps separate these two people and thus there are two intermediaries (John talks to Mary, Paul talks Sharon, and Sharon and Mary talk to one another).[14]

Personal network exposure can be computed by weighting exposure by the inverse of the geodesic for any two points. For example, the same individual represented in Figure 3.5 has five direct ties. Thus, he or she has five individuals who have a geodesic of one. He or she also has 15 individuals with whom he or she has a geodesic of two, that is, it takes two steps to reach each other.

The two-step indirect ties provide indirect network exposure to the innovation, and the degree of this exposure is weighted by the inverse of the number of steps. For example, the two-step indirect ties have a geodesic of two, and thus the weight of this exposure is one-half. The two-step indirect ties are summed and added to the direct ties to obtain a network exposure measure that is normalized so that personal network exposure still has a maximum of 100%.

The indirect influence of those who are three steps away, four steps away, and so on, can be computed. Theoretically, the degree of indirect influence can be extended to include the entire network. Unfortunately, each network has a different maximum number of geodesics: N-1. In some networks, everyone can reach everyone else in only a few steps; this is a highly connected network. In other networks, there may be as many as 10 or 15 steps required for every individual to reach every other individual. So, there is no method available to know how many steps along the geodesic need to be included to measure the influence of the whole network in a relational manner. Fortunately, research on flow networks provides a limiting case for how far to extend contagion influence.

---

[13]Consequently, for each time period, exposure may be positively associated with adoption. In other words, for each time period, those with higher exposure are more likely to adopt than those with low exposure. We test this model in Chapter 8.

[14]Lee (1977) has shown that generally adoption influence occurs through no more than two steps (i.e., one intermediary).

The flow matrix (Freeman, Borgatti, & White, 1991; see also Bogart, 1990; Ford & Fulkerson, 1962) represents the maximum amount of influence that can flow from any one individual to any other individual. Therefore, the flow matrix can be used to extend personal network exposure to include the relational influence of network adoption exposure for the whole network. The flow matrix is an N x N matrix whose elements represent the maximum amount of information that an individual can send to another individual. In other words, the flow matrix represents the degree of influence any individual has on any other individual in the network.

The data from any network study can be converted into a flow matrix. The conversion changes the network nominations matrix into a flow matrix. The flow matrix represents the broadest scope of influence we can use to model relational influence.

SUMMARY

The empirical results reported in this chapter are summarized in Table 3.2. These relational models demonstrate that innovativeness is influenced by the direct ties an individual sends and/or receives. If an individual receives many ties he or she is likely to adopt an innovation early because he or she is perceived as the system's opinion leader. An individual's direct ties also determine his or her group membership and although the present research showed little direct effect of group membership on adoption

Table 3.2. Summary of Empirical Findings for Relational Network Characteristics and Innovativeness.

| Relational Characteristic | Study Communities | | |
	Med. Innov.	Braz. Farm.	Korean Women
Opinion Leaders			
Received	.23**	.17***	.25***
Sent	.13	.01	.15***
Isolates	1.6 mos.	1.9 yrs.*	1.6 yrs.*
Density	.01	.03	.16
Radiality	.26**	.14***	.18***
Network Density			
Diffusion Rate	.97*	.61*	.49*
Saturation	-.17	-.12	.25

$^*p < .05;\ ^{**}p < .01;\ ^{***}p < .001$

behavior, in the extreme case of network isolation, isolates were found to be later adopters.

Additionally, direct ties determine whether an individual has access to information or knowledge about an innovation outside his or her immediate contacts. Individuals in dense networks do not readily receive information from outside their own social circle. Individuals who have radial networks, on the other hand, are more likely to hear about an innovation earlier because their network is more open to outside information.

Finally, a personal network exposure model was presented which posits that individuals are influenced to adopt an innovation by the proportion of their network that has adopted. It was shown that personal network exposure to an innovation increases during diffusion. In addition to direct ties as influences on adoption, the personal network exposure model can be expanded to include indirect ties through two or more intermediaries. The flow matrix was introduced which accounts for direct tie influences from the whole network.

The network exposure model expands the lens through which the individual monitors his or her direct contacts. The contagion process is extended from direct network ties to indirect ties of second or third degree and finally to the flow matrix. In this most general of all relational models, the diameter of an individual's social circle can be expanded to everyone in the system or contracted to only those with whom he or she has direct contact.

Relational models primarily analyze how an individual's direct contacts determine his or her adoption behavior. In contrast, structural models go beyond the set of direct nominations and consider the pattern of nominations in the whole network. Thus, the network influence on adoption for any individual cannot be determined by his or her nominations alone but must be considered in light of who everyone else in the network nominated.

In a sense, this is a false dichotomy because relation and structure are inevitably entwined. The crucial difference is that for structural models, the overall pattern of network nominations determines the position or role the individual has during the diffusion process. Thus, any individual's adoption behavior is seen through the behavior of the whole network.

Structural models try to determine how the structure of the social system influences diffusion of innovations. If, for example, diffusion occurred within groups how did innovations spread between groups? The next chapter addresses this question.

4

Structural Diffusion Networks

Structural models of diffusion postulate that the rate and character of diffusion are determined by structural characteristics of the social system within which the diffusion occurs. By the late 1960s and early 1970s, several schools of network analysis had developed (Scott, 1991). As network analysis increased in sophistication, so too did network models of diffusion. The first and perhaps most influential of this new set of network models of diffusion was Granovetter's strength of weak ties (SWT). Granovetter (1973, 1982) argued that weak ties—people loosely connected to others in the network—were necessary for diffusion to occur across subgroups within a system.

THE STRENGTH OF WEAK TIES

Granovetter's strength of weak ties was not specifically a theory of diffusion but rather a network theory. However, SWT is a network diffusion model although Granovetter did not build directly on prior network models of diffusion because he did not collect data about the diffusion of an innovation but rather collected data on how individuals obtained jobs. Granovetter postulated that weak ties, individuals loosely connected in a network, are bridges that serve to join unconnected groups (or cliques), thus acting as important links in the diffusion process.

Weak ties connect otherwise disconnected groups and act as a bridge for innovation diffusion. Without weak ties, diffusion is restricted to unconnected groups. Weak ties enable the innovation to be passed from one group within a network to another. Weak ties create more and shorter ties between individuals in a network, thus accelerating the rate of diffusion. "Intuitively speaking, this means that whatever is to be diffused can reach a larger number of people, and traverse greater social distance (i.e., path length), when passed through weak ties rather than strong" (Granovetter, 1978, p. 1366).

Recall Becker's (1970) contribution, reviewed in the previous chapter, that more advantageous innovations are adopted relatively earlier by centrals and less advantageous innovations are adopted relatively earlier by marginals. Granovetter's SWT argues that once the innovation is adopted by early adopters, weak ties are necessary to spread the innovation to the rest of the system. So it is not centrality or marginality that most strongly affects the rate of diffusion, rather it is the presence of weak ties.

Research by Kerckhoff, Back, and Miller (1965; Kerckhoff & Back, 1968) supported the role of marginals in adopting a controversial or risky innovation by showing that isolates (social marginals) were the first to "adopt" a case of social hysteria. Granovetter's SWT argued that risky innovations diffuse more quickly if they are adopted early by individuals with *many* weak ties. Risky innovations adopted early by individuals with *few* weak ties will have a slower rate of diffusion and will be confined initially to a few interconnected cliques (Granovetter, 1973, p. 1367).

Further support for the weak tie model exists in the "small world" studies by Milgram (Milgram, 1967; Travers & Milgram, 1969) and in the analysis of a large sociogram of junior high school students by Rapoport and Horvath (1961), both of which showed that weak ties are important behavioral influences. None of these studies, however, measured the existence of weak ties nor did they measure the contribution of weak ties to the rate of diffusion. In essence, a clear empirical analysis of the role of weak ties on diffusion has not been conducted.

Granovetter (1982) updated his review of weak tie applications. He referenced Fine and Kleinman (1979) on subcultures to show that subcultural norms emerge through the maintenance of weak ties. Granovetter also cited another small world experiment (Lin, Dayton, & Greenwald, 1977) and three science communication articles (Chubin, 1976; Collins, 1974; Friedkin, 1982) as further support for the weak tie model. Again, no network diffusion analysis was conducted to specifically test this argument, yet considerable tangential evidence for the important role of weak ties in the diffusion of innovations was presented.

Finally, Granovetter (1982) reviewed the study conducted by Weimann (1982) of the diffusion of rumors and gossip in an Israeli kibbutz, which was a network analysis of diffusion. It showed that marginals were important in relaying information throughout the group. Weimann's

study is the strongest evidence for the role of network weak ties in the diffusion process.

Weak ties are operationalized as the presence of individuals who
are likely to connect otherwise unconnected groups. These weak ties are
bridges, not weak because their strength is low, but because they connect
otherwise disconnected individuals. Radial individuals fulfill this role
because they have more network partners who nominate others outside
their personal network. To determine if weak ties accelerate diffusion the
average radiality index for each community was computed and correlated
with rate of adoption for the communities.

The results show that weak ties were not associated with more
rapid diffusion (correlations: medical innovation, -.44, p = ns; Brazilian
farmers, .04, p = ns; and Korean women, -.33, p = ns). These results
should not be taken as conclusive because the sample sizes are very small,
and it may be that radiality is a poor measure of the weak tie concept. A
full study would require considerable more attention to the role weak ties
play in each network and require that diffusion rates be compared for
identical networks with and without weak tie individuals. The results do
indicate that weak ties may not be as strong an influence on diffusion as is
usually considered.

Although the presence of weak ties may or may not accelerate diffusion between groups, there are other structural network characteristics
that may act as influences on the rate of diffusion. The most well-known
structural measure is centrality, which measures the degree to which an
individual receives many nominations and acts as a point of control in the
network (Bolland, 1988; Bonacich 1987a; Borgatti, Everett, & Freeman,
1992; Freeman, 1979; Stephenson & Zelen, 1989). Network centrality
may also contribute to the rate of diffusion by determining the degree to
which communication in the network is centralized in certain members
(Bonacich, 1987b).

CENTRALITY

In the previous chapter a model of opinion leadership was presented in
which individuals who received numerous nominations were more likely
to be earlier adopters of innovations. In essence, the opinion leader model
is a simplified model of the role of centrality in the diffusion of innovations. In the language of network analysis, opinion leaders, measured as
those receiving the most nominations, have a relatively high in-degree,
and their centrality in-degree measure is the highest in the network. *In-
degree* is the number of nominations received.

This is similar for the model of the number of nominations sent.

Individuals with a high number of nominations sent have high centrality out-degree. *Out-degree* is the number of nominations sent. But these measures were included in the chapter on relational models because they only consider the nominations received and sent by an individual. In contrast, there are other individual network centrality measures that consider the overall pattern of relations in the network and thus represent structural centrality measures. The two structural centrality measures to be considered are betweenness and closeness.

Centrality betweenness measures the degree an individual lies between other individuals on their paths to one another. The measure for betweenness centrality in a symmetric network is given in Freeman (1979, p. 224; SNAPS, 1989, p. 52):

$$2\sum_i \sum_j \frac{\frac{g_{ij}(p_k)}{g_{ij}}}{n2-3n+2}$$

in which g_{ij} represents the number of geodesics linking i and j and gij(pk) is the number of these geodesics that contain individual k. Centrality betweenness is a measure of how often an individual lies between the shortest path linking two other individuals. A high centrality betweenness indicates that the individual acts as an intermediary between many others in the network. It indicates that the individual is a possible relay between many potential communicants in the network and that the individual may broker many relationships.

Centrality closeness is the extent an individual is near other individuals in the network. An individual with high centrality closeness reaches others in the network more quickly, through fewer intermediaries, than others with lower centrality scores. Thus, closeness centrality individuals act as rapid conduits for an innovation because they are able to rapidly spread information and influence concerning the innovation to numerous others. The measure for closeness centrality in a symmetric network is given in Freeman (1979, p. 53; SNAPS, 1989, p. 52):

$$\frac{n-1}{\sum d_{ij}}$$

in which d_{ij} is the number of ties in the geodesic between i and j. Centrality closeness measures how many steps, on average, it takes for an individual to reach everyone else in the network. An individual with high closeness centrality has few steps between him- or herself and everyone else in the network. Both of these centrality measures are normalized so that they correct for the size of the network.

Individuals who are high in either of these centrality measures are more likely to receive information and influence concerning the innovation relatively earlier than others in the network. Therefore, these structural centrality measures should be associated with innovativeness. The correlations between betweenness centrality and innovativeness are: Medical innovation, .08 (p = ns); Brazilian farmers, .10 ($p < .05$); Korean family planning, .11 ($p < .001$). The correlations between closeness centrality and innovativeness are: Medical innovation, .09; (p = ns); Brazilian farmers, -.03 (p = ns); Korean family planning, .20 ($p < .001$).

These correlations indicate that structural centrality is weakly associated with earlier adoption by Korean women, less so for Brazilian farmers, and not at all for the doctors. The central positions are more likely to hear about the innovation earlier and be influenced to adopt the innovation earlier than those on the periphery. This is true in the Korean and Brazilian datasets, but not for the medical innovation dataset in which contagion was perhaps less a factor. Once the innovation is introduced, central members, by virtue of their position, hear about and receive influence about the innovation earlier, and thus are more likely to be early adopters. However, the effect is weak.

Network centrality is the degree that the links in a graph are concentrated in one or a group of individuals. A centralized network contains a few members who are the locus of contacts, whereas a decentralized network has the connections spread among many members in the network. Centralized networks have faster diffusion because once the innovation is adopted by a central member or members, it is more rapidly spread to the rest of the system. In a decentralized network, it takes longer for the innovation to reach everyone in the network.

Network centrality can be measured in a number of ways (Freeman, 1979). The two measures of individual centrality reviewed earlier have their network counterparts: network centralization betweenness and closeness. The correlations between centralization betweenness and rate of diffusion are: Medical innovation, .30 (p = ns); Brazilian farmers, -.19 (p = ns); Korean women, -.53 ($p < .01$).[1] The positive correlation for the medical innovation data and negative correlations for the Brazilian and Korean datasets indicate that network centrality is associated with more rapid diffusion when the innovation is perceived as more advantageous by members in the social system. However, in situations of greater risk/uncertainty, with slower diffusion, when the perceived advantageousness of the innovation is in question, centrality impedes diffusion.

The correlations between centralization betweenness and innova-

---

[1]Again, these correlations should be interpreted with some caution because the number of cases for each dataset is the number of communities and therefore represent small samples.

tion *prevalence* follow a similar pattern: Medical innovation, -.15 (p = ns); Brazilian farmers, -.71 ($p < .05$); Korean women, -.48 ($p < .05$). The negative correlations indicate that betweenness centralization tends to inhibit the innovation from reaching all members of the social system. In other words, betweenness centralization inhibits saturation; as the social system becomes more centralized, diffusion tends to reach fewer people in the network.

Closeness centralization follows a similar pattern: high negative correlations with rate and prevalence in the Brazil and Korea datasets, but insignificant correlations in the medical innovation data. Central networks are characterized by having communication directed at a few individuals. When an innovation is introduced, members of the system wait to see what the leaders, the central members, will do. For a relatively advantageous innovation, early adoption by central members of the system accelerates diffusion. However, for situations of greater risk/uncertainty, such as hybrid corn for farmers and family planning for rural women, centralization slows down the diffusion process and inhibits the innovation from being adopted by a greater proportion of the network.

Thus, the structure of the network, as measured by centrality, influences the diffusion of an innovation. For individuals, structural centrality is associated with innovativeness and for networks, structural centrality is associated with more rapid diffusion for advantageousness innovations and slower diffusion for more risky/uncertain innovations. Moreover, centralization tends to inhibit the innovation from reaching a greater proportion of adopters.

Weak ties and centrality represent two structural models that show that network structure may determine the rate of diffusion and the degree of prevalence. More specifically, weak ties and centrality represent models that postulate that the presence or absence of a certain kind of individual, a weak tie or central individual, impedes or facilitates diffusion. Another structural model of diffusion uses the role or positional structure of a network to determine whether individuals in the same position adopt innovations at about the same time.

POSITIONAL EQUIVALENCE

In the previous chapter, group membership on adoption was tested by determining whether individuals in the same group adopt innovations at about the same time. (In most cases groups did not have significantly different times of adoption.) Group membership was determined relationally by including individuals in a group if they were connected to one another. The structural analog to group membership is positional equivalence.

Positional equivalence is the degree two individuals are similar in their relations to all others in the network (Borgatti, Everett, & Freeman, 1992). Positional equivalence measures reduce a network to a set of positions so that two individuals who have the same set of relations to others in the network occupy the same position. Diffusion of innovations theory argues that individuals monitor the behavior of their near peers and are influenced by those who are similar to themselves. In other words, individuals imitate the adoption behavior of their near peers. Note that information is not necessarily directly communicated, but rather becomes more salient when those most like the individual engage in some behavior.[2] Therefore, individuals in the same position should adopt innovations at about the same time, and individuals in different positions should have different adoption times.

To test this hypothesis the CONCOR routine was applied to all 40 communities. CONCOR stands for converging correlations and is the process by which the columns of the matrix of network nominations are correlated with one another. This results in a matrix of correlations that is then used as input to correlate the columns, and so on. The CONCOR routine divides each network into two positions (Boorman & White, 1976; Brieger, Boorman, & Arabie, 1975; SNAPS, 1989; White, Boorman, & Brieger, 1976). Analysis of variance was then conducted to see if the average adoption times in the two positions were the same or different. If the average adoption times are the same, then the two positions do not influence innovation adoption.

Of the 40 communities, only 5 had significantly different adoption times between positions (Appendix C). Thus, this test does not show any influence of network position on adoption behavior. But this positional equivalence approach was not very comprehensive. In fact, positional analysis of innovation adoption is limited because every network will have different positional structures. Furthermore, positional equivalence does not provide a mechanism to determine which position, in general, influences which other positions. Moreover, it does not provide a mechanism to determine exactly who influences whom during the diffusion process. To resolve these problems, an individual measure of positional equivalence—structural equivalence—can be used.

STRUCTURAL EQUIVALENCE

Structural equivalence is the degree two individuals have the same relations with the same others (Burt, 1987; Lorrain & White, 1971; Sailer, 1978). In other words, structural equivalence is the degree two individuals

---

[2]Positional equivalence consists of role analysis that is a significant aspect of network analysis (Hummon & Carley, 1993).

occupy the same *position* in a social system. Individuals who occupy the same position monitor one another's behavior and consequently may adopt innovations at about the same time. A structural equivalence model of diffusion postulates that individuals are influenced to adopt an innovation by imitating the behavior of others to whom they are structurally equivalent. More importantly, the structural equivalence approach allows the specification of individual measures of equivalence rather than grouping all members of a position together.

Burt (1987) used structural equivalence in a reanalysis of the Coleman et al. (1966) medical innovation data. Burt eschewed a cohesion contagion model in favor of a contagion model that did not require direct contact between individuals. The equation for measuring structural equivalence (SE) is complicated because it considers the similarities in the distances two individuals have to every other individual in the network. For structural equivalence, each individual has a proximity measure that determines his or her degree of structural equivalence with every other individual. The equation for structural equivalence (SE) is:

$$SE_{ji} = \frac{(dmax_j - d_{ij})}{\sum_k (dmax_j - d_{kj})}$$

where:
$$d_{ij} = [(z_{ij} - z_{ji})^2 + \sum_k (z_{ik} - z_{jk})^2 + \sum_k (z_{ki} - z_{kj})^2]^{1/2}$$

in which Z_{ij} is the distance between the two points, computed as the geodesic between the two points.

Burt (1987) showed that weighting individuals by SE led to more accurate prediction of time of adoption than using direct ties. Personal network exposure based on direct ties for one individual (medical doctor from Peoria, identification number three) were presented in Figure 3.5. The SE weights for the same individual would be very difficult to display because it involves drawing a line and circle for every other doctor in the community—a total of 61 lines and circles. To compute personal network exposure based on structural equivalence, each other doctor's adoption would be multiplied by the SE weight, and these numbers added together. For the doctor in Figure 3.5, the structural equivalence network exposure values increase from .07 at time period one to .69 at time period 8 when he or she adopted. Note that the structural equivalence threshold, .69, is different (less than) the direct ties threshold, 1.0.

It is convenient to think of SE as a measure of similarity; the greater the structural equivalence, the more similar two individuals are. High SE indicates that two individuals are very similar in terms of their patterns of interactions with all others.

The advantage of structural equivalence over the positional approach presented in the previous section is that individual weights are assigned for each individual. In Chapter 3, a personal network exposure model was presented in which exposure was measured as the proportion of adopters in an individual's personal network. *SE network exposure* is the proportion of structurally equivalent adopters in an individual's personal network. As the innovation diffuses, more individuals adopt and thus provide SE network exposure to the innovation.

Burt's (1987) analysis of structural equivalence (SE) effects on diffusion was an extremely important piece of research that led to the realization of the different ways contagion can operate. In fact, Burt (1987) stated that simply using the SE weight matrix was not necessarily the best representation of SE's role in diffusion. The SE weights should be raised to a power that indicates the lens, the social radius of observation, that the individual uses to monitor the behavior of others. The exponentiation of the SE weight matrix, then, is the degree an individual is influenced by others near him or her in a structurally equivalent sense. Higher values of the exponent indicate that the individual is more sensitive to those who are near him or her.

To understand this process recall that SE is a measure that considers all contacts in the network. Therefore, for any two individuals in the network, an SE score exists between zero and one.[3] A high score indicates that the two are very similar in their relations with others in the network. By raising the SE weight to a power (greater than one) the relative influence of the larger SE scores is increased so that SE others have a greater influence on the individual.

The process of exponentiating the SE matrix to successive powers is analogous to the process described in the previous chapter for personal network exposure, but only in reverse. For personal network exposure via direct ties, the initial sphere of influence was the direct ties that were then extended along the geodesics (direct paths), and finally to the flow matrix. For SE, the initial SE matrix represents the broadest frame of reference, the largest sphere of influence, and successive integers of the exponent, referred to as v, shrink the social radius of influence.

The correlation between time of adoption and SE network exposure for four values of v (1, 4, 8, 16) and cohesion network exposure are presented in Table 4.1. Notice that the correlation decreases as the sphere of influence shrinks from the whole network to only those who are near the individual. These high correlations between time of adoption and SE-based

---

[3]An SE weight is close to zero because the sum of all SE weights for an individual is equal to one. In other words, each individual has an SE score with everyone else in the network. The sum of these scores is one. The proportion for any one individual is the degree of structural equivalence.

Table 4.1. Correlation Between Time of Adoption and 11 Network Threshold Measures.

	Combined N = 1790	Drug Study N = 119	Brazilian Farmers N = 646	Korean Fam Pl. N = 1025
Coh: 1st Noms	.44	.60	.51	.65
Coh: 2nd Noms	.47	.62	.65	.68
Coh: 3rd Noms	.55	.73	.74	.78
Coh: Flow Net	.61	.79	.78	.84
SE: v=1	.65	.95	.87	.94
SE: v=4	.65	.95	.87	.94
SE: v=8	.29	.52	.65	.74
SE: v=16	-.03	.25	.50	.30
Coh: Closeness Centrality	.47	.62	.62	.68
Struct: Between				
Centrality	.44	.57	.59	.59
Multiplexity	.47	.62	.62	.66

Note: All correlations significant at $p < .001$.

network exposure are simply an artifact of using adoption as a weight matrix. We analyze the competing network exposure models, direct ties versus SE and near versus far influences, in the following chapters.

RELATIONAL VS. STRUCTURAL

Clearly, a tradition of diffusion networks research has developed over the past 30 years to more clearly examine the conclusion by Ryan and Gross (1943) that diffusion occurs through social contacts. However laudable this research is, it falls short in a number of ways. The shortcomings are due to paradigmatic blinders as well as resulting from the difficulty of collecting and analyzing diffusion network data.

Relational and structural network models of the diffusion of innovations both show that network relations and network positions influence adoption behavior. The relational models start from the direct ties an individual has in a network and show how this influences adoption behavior. In contrast, structural models start from the pattern of all relations in the network and show how this influences adoption behavior. In many cases, predictions from the relational and structural approaches are likely to be similar. That is, individuals who are central are also likely to be in the same position and hence have similar adoption times.

Indeed, when relational contagion exists, one is also likely to find structural contagion. Tension between relational and structural approaches is only to be found when the pattern of nominations is such that individuals who are linked directly occupy dissimilar positions in the social space. Such conditions are rather rare. What remains to be done, then, is to determine how relational and structural perspectives complement or compete with one another. In Figure 1.4, we presented a diagram of contagion influences. The preceding analysis has not provided an adequate means to differentiate the two sets of influence.

The principal problem with the network models presented earlier is that they do not provide an integrating framework within which to compare relational versus structural influences. Both the relational and structural models developed thus far are treated in isolation without the possibility of comparing one with the other. There is no way to compare group membership based on direct ties with positional equivalence as influences on adoption.

Moreover, these models fail to specify the exact flow of influence in the network to determine exactly who influences whom during the diffusion process. The two-step flow hypothesis cannot, thus far, specify exactly which opinion leaders influence which opinion followers. This often happens because network models specify that individuals should have similar adoption times without specifying who should adopt earlier and who should adopt later.

A general network model that can compare relational and structural influences is presented in the following chapters. The model builds on the personal network perspective and permits the comparison of relational and structural weights on personal network exposure. Personal network exposure, both in the relational and positional perspectives, represents the most general case of all the models reviewed earlier.

When contagion is limited to the immediate social circle, the individual's smallest sphere of influence, relational personal network exposure is the set of direct ties, and structural equivalence network exposure is the SE weight matrix raised to a higher power. Expanding the sphere of influence permits the inclusion of indirect ties in the relation case, and less SE others in the positional case. Expanding the sphere of contagion still further approximates the effects of groups and roles, and finally, the limiting case for both relational and structural perspectives permits the inclusion of the whole network.

The personal network exposure model provides a mechanism for modeling contagion in both the kind (direct ties vs. positional equivalence) and degree of lens (near vs. far) used by the individual to monitor social influence. Network exposure by itself is insufficient for this task. Exposure is highly correlated with time of adoption because it is measured with time of adoption. To use network exposure we need to determine when exposure is effective at influencing adoption. Thus, we turn to thresholds, which is the subject of the next chapter.

SUMMARY

In sum, a set of structural models of diffusion exist that argue that the structure of the social system determines the rate of diffusion. Empirical results from the structural tests are presented in Table 4.2. The first structural model presented was the weak tie approach, which specified that individuals who are weakly connected to groups in a network serve an important function by permitting an innovation to diffuse between groups.

The centrality of individuals and their networks were also shown to have significant effects on the rate of diffusion. High individual structural centrality measures (betweenness and closeness) resulted in individuals becoming aware of the innovation earlier and being influenced by other adopters earlier. Hence structural centrality is positively associated with innovativeness. Network centrality was shown to be associated with the rate of diffusion. Centralized networks slowed the rate of diffusion and restricted its spread when the innovation was uncertain/risky.

Table 4.2. Summary of Empirical Findings for Structural Network Characteristics and Innovativeness.

Structural Characteristic	Study Communities		
	Med. Innov.	Braz. Farm.	Korean Women
Weak Ties	.44	-.04	.33
Centrality			
Betweenness	.08	.10*	.11***
Closeness	.09	-.03	.20***
Network Centrality Betweenness			
Rate	.30	-.19	-.53**
Prevalence	-.15	-.71*	-.48*
Network Centrality Closeness			
Rate	.53	.01	-.25
Prevalence	-.04	-.76**	-.29

$*p < .05; **p < .01; ***p < .001$

A positional equivalence model was constructed in which individuals in the same position were hypothesized to adopt innovations at about the same time. The results showed that individuals in the same position did not adopt at about the same time. Finally, a structural equivalence model of diffusion was presented that argued that positional equivalence can be operationalized so that individuals receive a measure that determines how similar they are without putting them in positions. The structural equivalence model permitted more exact specification of contagion via structural equivalence and represents a generic structural weighting scheme.

Finally, the tension between relational and structural models and the failure of these perspectives to be adequately compared was discussed. A general model of network diffusion using personal network exposure provides the best means to compare various network diffusion models. The personal network exposure model, however, requires a better understanding of thresholds in the diffusion of innovations.

Threshold Models
of Diffusion

This chapter reviews prior research on threshold models of the diffusion of innovations. The first section provides an introduction to threshold models that have been applied to a wide variety of phenomenon through computer simulations, yet, to date, have not been applied to real-life situations. The second section presents a network threshold model. Advantages and disadvantages of the personal network threshold are discussed as is the appropriateness for using personal network thresholds versus group or system thresholds.

The second section also presents some empirical findings using the network threshold model. Threshold lags are presented in the third section. Lags occur because there is a delay in threshold activation such that network exposure may reach the threshold level at a point in time earlier than the actual time of adoption. Factors that reduce threshold lags include media campaigns and cosmopoliteness. Finally, a structural network threshold measure and some empirical results are presented in the last section.

THRESHOLD MODELS

Granovetter (1978) initiated[1] research on thresholds in the diffusion of innovations by postulating that individuals were not homogenous in the degree they were influenced by their social system. In other words, indi-

---

[1]Hägerstrande (1967) postulated a relationship between a resistance distribution and rate of diffusion. Hägerstrande concluded "the higher the resistance the more concentrated the distribution [of adopters]" (p. 272).

viduals differ in the degree they are influenced by the behavior of others in their social system. For example, some individuals engage in a riot when few others have done so, yet others wait until almost everyone has rioted before joining in.

Threshold models (Granovetter, 1978; Granovetter & Soong, 1983, 1986, 1988) generally assume that individuals have varying thresholds for adoption of an innovation. Individuals have low, medium, or high thresholds, and it is the distribution of thresholds in a social system that determines the rate of diffusion. The heterogeneity of thresholds is postulated as one cause of individual differences in time of adoption. Hence, individuals can be classified as low or high threshold adopters in addition to being classified as early or late adopters.

The threshold model is based on the proposition that earlier adoption occurs for those individuals with lower thresholds, and later adoption occurs for those with higher thresholds. Low thresholds are synonymous with low resistance (and earlier adoption within a group), whereas high thresholds are synonymous with high resistance (and with later adoption within a group). Typically, thresholds are assumed to be normally distributed, thus resulting in a cumulative distribution function (CDF) when cumulative adoption is plotted over time as in Figure 1.1 (the CDF is similar in shape to the logistic function).

The degree an individual is influenced by others in his or her social system is an individual's threshold. For example, in a potential riot situation (Granovetter, 1978), a number of people may be milling around a square. An individual with a zero threshold will engage in a riot before anyone else, thus initiating the riot. An individual with a threshold of 1 sees this first person engage in riot behavior and then begins to riot him- or herself. The process snowballs as more individuals reach their threshold and join the riot. The threshold curve is shown in Figure 5.1.

Granovetter (1978) defined an individual's threshold as "the proportion of the group he would have to see join before he would do so" (p. 1422). Individuals vary in their propensity to riot depending on a number of predispositional variables that determine the individual's cost of being apprehended and the perceived benefits of rioting. Thus, a more formal definition of an individual's *threshold* is the point at which the perceived benefits exceed the perceived costs (Granovetter, 1978, p. 1422).

Granovetter (1978) provided numerous examples of threshold effects such as strikes, educational attainment, and leaving social situations such as lectures, migration, and experimental social psychology. The threshold model for each of these situations, and many of those reviewed in Chapter 2, postulates that individuals make decisions (adopt/not adopt, leave/stay, vote for/vote against) based on the proportion of others that have already done so. The threshold model does not determine how these

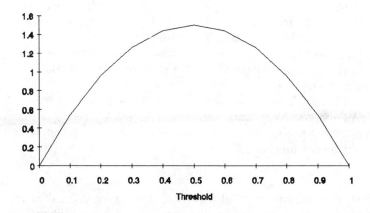

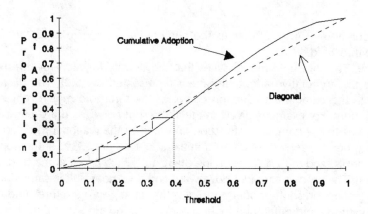

Figure 5.1. The threshold density function yields a polynomial cumulative diffusion pattern

Note: The threshold density function is the distribution of thresholds for an innovation. The height of the curve has no substantive interpretation. The distribution represented by $6(y)$ $(1-y)$, in which y is the cumulative number of adopters at a given point in time, yields the s-shaped curve represented by polynomial $3x^2-2x^3$. The normal density function of thresholds does not reach saturation unless some other force persuades individuals with low thresholds to adopt.

thresholds are obtained, that is, it avoids determining the sociopsychological determinants of an individual's threshold.

The threshold model argues that individuals decide to engage in a behavior such as adopting an innovation depending on the proportion of prior adopters in the social system. An individual's threshold is a function of personal and social factors that combine to determine how many people in a system must engage in a behavior before an individual is willing to engage in that behavior (also see Schelling, 1978).

In general, thresholds are assumed to have the distribution represented by the density function shown in Figure 5.1. The density function for thresholds represents the distribution of thresholds in a population. The threshold density function is:

$$y = 6(x)(1-x) \qquad (5.1)$$

in which x is the number of adopters at a given point in the diffusion. The function describing cumulative adoption is given by the integral of (5.1) which is:

$$y = 3x^2 - 2x^3 \qquad (5.2)$$

The polynomial in (5.2) defines the cumulative number of adopters for a given threshold.

The threshold model states that the density function for thresholds yields the cumulative adoption pattern represented by (5.2). The diagonal through the cumulative adoption curve for the threshold model represents equilibrium. For example, given an initial threshold of 40%, draw a line from the x-axis to the cumulative function and then to the diagonal to determine the number of adopters. With 40% initial adopters, only 33% of the population adopts, and with 33% adopting, then only 25% adopt at the next time interval. The process cascades downward and does not result in saturation.

The threshold model postulates that changes in the threshold density function yield different adoption patterns. If the threshold density function is skewed right, diffusion occurs more rapidly. If the threshold density function is skewed left, diffusion occurs more slowly. The threshold density function skewed right, presented in Figure 5.2, represents the case when more individuals have lower thresholds. That is, more individuals are likely to adopt an innovation after seeing few others adopt.

The cumulative adoption curve for thresholds skewed right does reach saturation by the cascading process described above. For example, given an initial threshold of 40%, if we draw a line to the cumulative function and then to the diagonal we see that 60% will adopt. The process cascades upward until saturation.

The threshold density function skewed left, presented in Figure 5.3, represents the case when more individuals have high thresholds. That is, more individuals are likely to adopt an innovation only after seeing many others adopt. Figure 5.3 shows a hypothetical threshold density

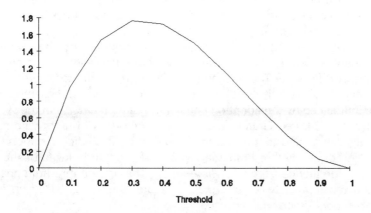

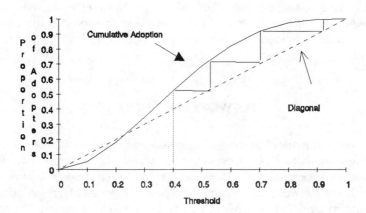

Figure 5.2. The threshold density function skewed right and its diffusion pattern

Note: The threshold density skewed right indicates that more individuals are likely to adopt an innovation after seeing *few* others adopt. The hypothetical density function skewed right has a cumulative adoption pattern represented by the polynomial $6x^2-8x^3+3x^4$. The density function skewed right has a more rapid diffusion. The density function skewed right reaches saturation.

function skewed left and its diffusion pattern. Thresholds skewed left do not reach saturation by the threshold process alone; some other influence such as a drop in price, an advertising campaign, role modeling, cosmopolitan contact and so on must be present to reduce thresholds so they become skewed right.

The threshold model of diffusion, as formulated by Granovetter, is not a network model per se, but it does have implications for network models of diffusion.[2] The threshold model is applicable to network diffusion models because it postulates that individuals vary in their propensity to be influenced by the adoption behavior of other members in the system. Dozier (1977) tested Granovetter's threshold model with a forward recursion algorithm[3] and found that the model did not predict adoption well. However, this early threshold analysis considered thresholds to be the proportion of influence *from the whole group*. The present threshold analysis constructed from network information creates thresholds based on influence *from one's personal network*.

Network thresholds permit exact specification of the individual influence process present during the diffusion process. An initial network threshold model was tested by Rice and others (1990) in an organizational setting. They classified individual adopters of an electronic mail system according to whether they used the system and showed that the connectedness of an individual is associated with adoption of an electronic mail system.

NETWORK THRESHOLDS

The threshold model has intuitive appeal and has been buttressed by considerable mathematics. However, prior threshold research omitted the influence of personal network dynamics. Threshold models assumed that the personal network of a potential adopter influenced his or her adoption in a *static* manner. The network was perceived to be a static influence on the potential adopter, and individuals were assumed to have the same proportion of adopters and nonadopters in their personal network. Prior threshold models argued that individual heterogeneity of thresholds accounted for different adoption times, yet did not consider heterogeneity of network position. In other words, prior research assumed that personal networks did not change over time.

---

[2]Granovetter (1978) did suggest the possibility of using sociomatrices as weights on individual adoption decisions (p. 1429), but he specifically eschewed a contagion model (p. 1423). I believe this is because, at that time, contagion was not viewed in as broad a context as this book postulates, and the analytical tools were not yet developed.

[3]The forward recursion algorithm used the proportion of adopters at time t to predict an individual's adoption at time t+1 (Dozier, 1977).

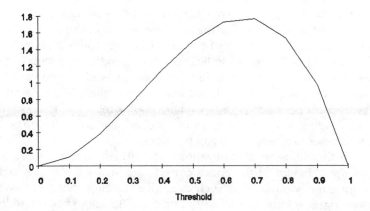

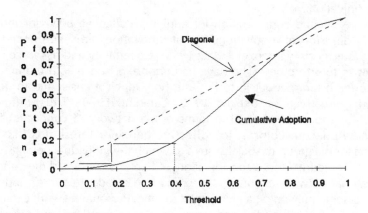

Figure 5.3. The threshold density function skewed left and its diffusion pattern

Note: The threshold density skewed left indicates that more individuals are likely to adopt an innovation after seeing *many* others adopt. They hypothetical density function skewed right has a cumulative adoption pattern represented by the polynomial $4x^3-3x^4$. The density function skewed left has a slower diffusion. The density function skewed left does not reach saturation unless some other force persuades individuals to adopt such as the media, role modeling, and so on.

The reason prior threshold models ignored personal network influences is that most of the applications of threshold models came from collective action examples. However, as mentioned in Chapter 1, collective action and diffusion are different situations and thus provide opportunities to expand theories from each. Threshold model applications of the diffusion of innovations must consider the roles of observability and uncertainty. *Observability* is the degree individuals may witness the adoption experiences of others. In collective action situations, individuals generally have complete information concerning the behavior of others in the social system. Everyone's behavior is observable. In instances such as riots, street crossing, leaving a lecture, and so on, individuals are able to see and know what everyone else in the group is doing.

In the diffusion of innovations, individuals may not accurately monitor the behavior of the entire group, particularly for an innovation that is not directly observable, such as family planning, bottle or newspaper recycling, opinions, and so forth. In these diffusion examples, individuals do not know the adoption behavior of everyone else in the group and therefore must receive information about others' behavior based on direct communication.

A second consideration for applying collective behavior thresholds to diffusion of innovations is that innovations are often uncertain, ambiguous, or risky (Menzel & Katz 1955). Uncertainty and risk force individuals to turn to others who have had prior experience with the innovation to learn more about it, to find out how much it costs, and to determine its effectiveness (Becker, 1970; Cancian, 1979). Thus, diffusion thresholds should be defined in terms of the network of connections for the individual, in contrast to collective behavior thresholds that are defined for the group or social system to which the individual belongs.

To address these considerations, Chapter 3 presented the concept of *personal network exposure*, the proportion of adopters in an individual's personal network at a given point in time. Personal network exposure addresses the observability and uncertainty considerations and measures the *dynamic* quality of personal networks. Personal network exposure levels increase over time as more individuals adopt the innovation, and they vary across individuals according to whom they nominate in the network.

A collective behavior threshold is the proportion of prior adopters in a group which is appropriate for collective behaviors, such as a riot, because everyone's behavior is observable (and thus information is complete). However, because adoption of innovations is not always observable and often involves risk, it is more likely to be a function of direct communication and persuasion between network partners. Therefore, diffusion *thresholds* are the proportion of prior adopters in an individual's personal network of direct personal contacts when the individual adopts.

The lens through which individuals monitor the behavior of others can be varied in the case of diffusion of innovations. The social sphere of reference can be reduced to individuals who are linked directly or who are very near one another in status. Because innovations are often unobservable, risky, and/or uncertain, closer contact is necessary for the individual to receive information and be influenced by the adoption behavior of others.

In collective action, or other social change processes, individuals may very well monitor the whole group, weighting every individual's behavior equally, or simultaneously weighing near partners more and distant partners less. Prior modeling has assumed group influence without varying the lens of observability for individuals. The personal network exposure model permits variation of the influence sphere as well as the selection of which others influence an individual's behavior.

PERSONAL NETWORK EXPOSURE

In Chapter 3, a personal network exposure model was presented in which individuals are exposed to the innovation by their direct contacts (Figure 3.5). Personal network exposure provides a direct operationalization of individual diffusion thresholds by conceptualizing the frame of reference to be an individual's immediate peers rather than the whole social system. Notice that the definition of thresholds is the same; the point at which benefits outweigh costs to adoption. However, for diffusion, *the frame of reference has changed to include only the role of immediate peers, the individual's intimate social sphere.* Thus, for diffusion, an individual's threshold is the proportion of an individual's personal network who must adopt before he or she does, and *thresholds are the exposure level necessary for an individual to adopt an innovation.*

Recall the example in Figure 3.5 in which the doctor's exposure increased from zero to one through contact with five other doctors. When the doctor adopted, his or her personal network exposure was one, therefore his or her threshold was one. In this example, the doctor adopts after all the people in his or her personal network have adopted, resulting in a threshold of one (or 100%). If the doctor had adopted when his or her personal network exposure was 70% his or her threshold would be .7 because 70% of his or her network was necessary for him or her to adopt.

The proportion of adopters in an individual's personal network generally increases during diffusion because over time more individuals adopt the innovation. The increase in the proportion of adopters in the individuals' personal networks does not occur uniformly in the system, but rather increases according to the structure of the system defined by the pattern of communication in the network. In other words, everyone's personal network eventually fills with adopters, yet some personal networks fill earlier than others, as defined by the adoption behavior of their network partners.

Exposure[4] is the proportion of adopters in an individual's personal network at a point in time. Exposure is computed by multiplying the matrix of social network nominations by the adoption vector for each time period and then dividing by the vector of the number of nominations made by each respondent. Thus, the equation for exposure is:

$$E_{nt} = \frac{S_{nn} \times A_{nt}}{S_{n+}} \tag{5.3}$$

in which E is the exposure matrix, S is the social network, A is the adoption matrix, n is the number of respondents, $n+$ indicates the sum of each row, and t is the time period. The exposure equation is a very general model in which the social network can be direct relations, positional relations, narrowly or broadly focused. Thresholds are then computed from exposure by using the time-of-adoption vector to create a design matrix that is multiplied by the exposure matrix (Appendix A presents the Gauss program written to compute exposure and thresholds).

For example, consider the diffusion of modern family planning practices in a developing country. Prior threshold models assumed that village women in Korea had varying thresholds for adopting modern family planning methods (Dozier, 1977; Rogers & Kincaid, 1981). Some women adopt family planning regardless of how many others adopt, whereas other women adopt if half of their village adopts, and still others adopt only if everyone else has adopted. These three collective behavior thresholds are 0%, 50%, and 100%, respectively.

The personal network threshold model states that these women are influenced to adopt family planning by the proportion of their personal network partners who also adopt (family planning). In a village of 100 women who might adopt family planning, a woman may be connected through family or friendship ties to 10 of them, and she is influenced by the percentage of her 10 network partners who do or do not adopt family planning. Thus, of the 100 women in the village, the individual communicates with 10 and decides to use family planning based on the proportion of these 10 who adopt. If 6 of the 10 adopt, then exposure is 60% (6/10 = 0.6) and if she adopts when her exposure is 0.6, then she has a threshold of 0.6.

Notice that in the present example, exposure changes as more people adopt and that exposure varies according to whom each individual is connected to in the social system. The contagion model states that individuals adopt based on the degree of exposure to the innovation; the social network structures that exposure. The exposure received may or may not result in adoption, depending on an individual's threshold. Figure

---

[4]I am indebted to Phil Bonacich for suggesting the term exposure (see also Rice, 1993; Rice & Aydin 1991), which helps imply a direct analogy to epidemics.

5.4 displays the network thresholds for the Korean family planning data.

The average threshold value for the Korean dataset is .57 (*SD* = .38) which indicates that the women of this sample, on average, wait until 57% of their network uses family planning before they are willing to do so. If we drop nonadopters (i.e., examine thresholds only for those who adopted), the average is .45 (*SD* = .34). The correlation for thresholds and time of adoption is .57 (*p* < .001) which indicates a strong association between time of adoption and network thresholds.

Personal network thresholds are also highly correlated with time of adoption in the medical innovation data (*r* = .5 ; *p* < .001) and in the Brazilian farmers data (*r* = .5; *p* < 001). Indeed, because exposure is computed from the adoption times of others in the network, it is not surprising that thresholds are correlated with adoption. However, the correlation is far from 100%, indicating that many individuals have different network and system thresholds, and in Chapter 7 we combine system and network thresholds.

Network thresholds may also be associated with external contact variables such as cosmopoliteness and media consumption for the three datasets. The correlations between network thresholds and the number of medical journals received (-.09; *p* = ns); farmers visits to nearest large city (-.13; *p* < .001); and Korean women's media campaign exposure (-.03; *p* = ns) are weak and generally not significant. However, Chapter 7 shows that network thresholds are useful in explaining the pattern of the diffusion of innovations and the influence of these external contact variables.

Although there is a danger in constructing one variable from another, there are considerable advantages to the threshold concept. Past diffusion research has always operationalized the concept of innovative-

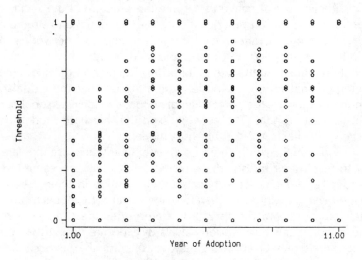

Figure 5.4. Thresholds for the Korean family planning dataset

ness as time of adoption (Rogers, 1983; Ryan & Gross, 1943). Early adopters were considered innovative and a host of variables were discovered to be related to innovativeness including education, income, cosmopoliteness, and opinion leadership.

The threshold concept enables us to determine innovativeness relative to the social system *and* relative to personal networks. The degree of overlap between system and personal network innovativeness measures true innovativeness. Some individuals may be innovative with respect to the system, yet not with respect to their personal network. Those who are innovative with respect to both system and personal networks are truly innovative. The distinction between system and individual-level innovativeness also helps clarify the diffusion process. For example, income is highly associated with early adoption, indicating that individuals with higher levels of income generally adopt innovations earlier. This is not surprising because individuals with higher income have less risk when purchasing a new product or investing in new equipment. Suppose income is not associated with personal network thresholds. This indicates that income is not associated with individual-level innovativeness and hence does not lead individuals to adopt early relative to their peers.

A stronger association between income and system-level innovativeness rather than personal network innovativeness would indicate that income does not make individuals more innovative per se, but rather provides some structural access to resources or information not available to those with less income. In other words, income does not make one more innovative relative to his or her peers because one's peers probably have the same income, but rather more innovative relative to the social system.

In sum, social networks capture the structure of the social system that influences diffusion of innovations. Both relational and structural perspectives can be operationalized through a model of network exposure that influences adoption. Prior threshold models argued that the threshold distribution influenced the rate of diffusion. The present threshold model is an interpersonal influence model which argues that individuals adopt when their exposure, the percentage of adopters in their personal network, reaches their threshold. The network exposure threshold model incorporates network effects into the threshold model.

Individuals with high exposure adopt early because they are more likely to reach their threshold. Thus, individuals with the same threshold may adopt at different times because their position in their network dictates their level of exposure. Therefore, the social network determines individual exposure and the threshold determines the time of adoption. Because individuals have various levels of exposure during the course of diffusion, there may be some lag between the time their exposure reaches their threshold and their adoption time. That is, for some individuals there exists a lag period in which there is no change in their personal network exposure and the time of adoption.

THRESHOLD LAGS

A *threshold lag* is the number of time periods between the time when an individual's exposure reaches his or her threshold and his or her time of adoption. Threshold lags occur because individuals are not immediately influenced by their peers, but may continually monitor their behavior. The network exposure may not be sufficient to induce behavior change until some "cue to action" or trigger event occurs to activate an individual's threshold.

The example of income was used to demonstrate the difference between innovativeness relative to peers versus innovativeness relative to the social system. Income should be negatively associated with threshold lags because lack of resources is a barrier to adoption. So, once an individual's threshold exposure is met, the lag in adoption will be reduced by the available monies to buy the innovation.

For example, individual 48 in the Korean family planning village number 24 adopted family planning at time period 7 with a threshold of 60% (three out of five nominations). However, this individual had a threshold lag of 3 which indicates that she waited 3 years between the time her exposure reached 60% and the time she adopted. In other words, in 1966 three of her five network partners had adopted family planning, however, she waited another three years, until 1969, to adopt family planning herself. During those three years there was no change in her personal network's adoption activity.[5]

The threshold lag has a skewed distribution because it is a function of time of adoption. That is, everyone is eligible to have a lag of zero; however, individuals who adopt at time period one may not have lags greater than zero, and individuals who adopt at time period two may have lags of zero and one, but not greater than one. Consequently the threshold lag distribution may have many values of zero, fewer of one, fewer of two, and so on up to the last time period of adoption, which will have the fewest number of cases. Figure 5.5 presents the threshold lag distribution for the Korean family planning dataset.

The magnitude of the threshold lags indicates the degree of delay in threshold activation. What factors are likely to create threshold lags? Disincentives to adoption, such as high cost, will cause delays in threshold activation and yield higher lag values. Conversely, positive inducements, such as rebates, will decrease thresholds, inducing individuals to adopt at

---

[5]There is a second type of threshold lag that cannot be measured in the current framework, but it is nonetheless present. This lag occurs when an individual reaches his or her threshold, but does not adopt the innovation, *and* his or her network exposure continues to increase.

their threshold. For example, media campaigns may act as "cues to action" or triggers that induce adoption of some prosocial behaviors.

Reanalysis of the diffusion datasets supports the argument that media campaigns reduce threshold lags. Exposure to media sources (Brazilian farmers) and a media campaign (Korean family planning) resulted in lower threshold lags. Specifically, the correlation between the threshold lag and the number of media sources was -.16 ($p < .001$) for the Brazilian farmers. The correlation between the threshold lag and the media campaign score was -.23 ($p < .001$) for the Korean women.[6] Thus, media persuasion decreased threshold lags resulting in earlier threshold activation.

STRUCTURAL NETWORK THRESHOLDS

The personal network threshold can also be used to include structural properties of the network in order to compare various formulations of network models of diffusion. Chapter 3 presented relational models of diffusion such as the opinion leader framework, which argued that opinion leaders of innovations are earlier adopters, and opinion followers imitate the behavior of leaders. To test this hypothesis, network exposure to an

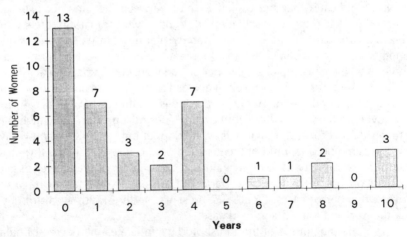

Figure 5.5. Threshold lags for Korean family planning village 24

Note: Threshold lags represent the number of time periods between the time an individual's exposure first reaches the threshold level and the eventual time of adoption. A lag of zero indicates no delay, whereas a lag of three indicates three time periods (in the present case years) between exposure reaching the threshold and time of adoption.

[6]This result persisted when controlling for time of adoption, which indicates that the correlation is not spurious stemming from the lag's correlation with time of adoption.

innovation can be weighted by the opinion leadership scores (number of nominations) to get a more accurate measure of the role of interpersonal influence during diffusion.

Opinion leaders are hypothesized to have more influence in the flow of information and persuasion about an innovation. Individuals who nominate opinion leaders should thus be more influenced by these opinion leaders when deciding to adopt an innovation. Consequently, the level of exposure is increased by the opinion leadership of the nominees and thresholds for individuals in the network can be computed from the resulting exposure matrix.

Additionally, an individual's exposure can be weighted by the centrality scores of individuals in the network. Central members of the network are hypothesized to have greater influence during the diffusion of an innovation. Weighting exposure by centrality scores for individuals captures this higher level of influence. Thresholds can then be computed from the centrality weighted exposures.

The most parsimonious structural measure discussed in Chapter 4 was structural equivalence (SE), which provides measures for how similar two individuals are structurally in the network. SE weights measure proximity in social space in which high scores indicate that two individuals are similar in terms of their interactions with others in the network.

Personal network exposure scores were computed from the SE matrix to model the influence SE others have on adoption of innovations. SE thresholds were then computed from the SE personal exposure measures. The SE network thresholds range from zero to one, in which a low SE threshold indicates an individual who adopted before most of his or her SE others adopted, and a high SE threshold indicates an individual who adopted after his or her SE others adopted.

SE network thresholds are also associated with external contact variables such as cosmopoliteness and media consumption. The correlations between SE network thresholds and the number of medical journals received (-.05; p = ns); visits to nearest large city (-.09; p < .05); and media campaign exposure (-.11; p < .001) are weak (yet two out of three are significant at the usually accepted probability levels), like those for cohesion network thresholds.

Note that the correlation for media campaign exposure is strongly significant when it was not significant for cohesion thresholds. Thus, network thresholds open up the possibility of comparing different network models of diffusion and their results. Here we see that media exposure is associated with innovativeness relative to structurally equivalent others and not with innovativeness relative to those with whom the Korean women are in direct contact.

SUMMARY

The threshold model was developed to explain how collective behaviors such as riots, strikes, voting behavior, and diffusion of innovations occur. Specifically, the threshold model explained how two seemingly similar situations can result in one reaching a collective goal and the other not reaching the goal. The models asserted that an individual's threshold is the proportion of a group needed to engage in a behavior before an individual will do so.

The present chapter argues that such a conceptualization of thresholds may be appropriate for collective action because everyone's behavior in the group is observable. However, for the diffusion of innovations, which is often characterized by unobservability, risk, and uncertainty, thresholds should be conceptualized as the proportion of an individual's network needed to adopt a behavior before an individual would do so.

Individual exposure to an innovation increases as more people in one's personal network adopt the innovation. Individuals who adopt before anyone else in their network have zero thresholds, whereas individuals who adopt after most of their network has adopted have high thresholds. Note that individuals with the same threshold may adopt at different times because their personal network partners' behavior influences their level of exposure. Finally, various network exposure weighting schemes were presented that model relational and structural influences on adoption of innovations.

In addition to exposure and threshold influences there is also a system-level influence on an individual's decision to adopt an innovation. The system-level influence is the proportion of the social system that have adopted an innovation at a given point in time. The cumulative adoption of an innovation reaches a critical mass when enough adopters exist to propel diffusion.

Critical Mass
Models of Diffusion

The critical mass is a powerful metaphor and convenient phrase often used in a *deus ex machina*[1] manner to solve theoretical discussions. The present chapter reviews the various definitions of the critical mass in the literature which, like thresholds, spans many disciplines. Reaching the critical mass is often a stated goal of both social and product marketing campaigns. This chapter provides an understanding of the critical mass and indications of how and where to find it.

The critical mass in collective action has received the most attention from Oliver and Marwell (1988; Marwell, Oliver, & Prahl, 1988; Oliver, Marwell, & Teixeira, 1985; Prahl, Marwell, & Oliver, 1991) and Macy (1990, 1991). In communication, the critical mass has been studied by Rogers (1991), Rice (Rice, 1990; Rice et al. 1990), Markus (1987), Allen (1988), and others. The first section of this chapter discusses inflection points as a means to understanding the critical mass. The second section presents network definitions of the critical mass. The third section provides techniques for measuring the critical mass and evaluating the potential for finding it.

The *critical mass* is a system-level measure of the minimum number of participants needed to sustain a diffusion process.[2] For example, a

---

[1]Deus ex machina (latin for god from a machine) refers to the practice in Greek and Roman drama of introducing a deity by stage machinery to intervene in a difficult situation, often to untangle a complicated plot.

[2]In physics, the critical mass is defined as the amount of radioactive material needed to sustain a chain-reaction explosion with a mass of explosive material.

riot reaches critical mass when enough individuals have begun rioting to insure that the riot spreads. An epidemic reaches critical mass when the proportion of sick people in a population is so high that the epidemic spreads and all those not immune become ill. But these vague notions of the critical mass do not specify which individuals constitute a critical mass or what proportion of adopters qualifies as the critical mass.

INFLECTION POINTS

The critical mass may be equated with inflection points. An *inflection point* occurs when a curve "bends," that is, when a curve increases or decreases most rapidly. The curve for the diffusion of an innovation is shown in Figure 6.1, with a first-order inflection point and two second-order inflection points. The *first-order inflection point* occurs when the rate of adoption is fastest. It is the peak in the first derivative of the logistic function and occurs when the second derivative equals zero. The *second-order inflection point* occurs when the rate of the rate of adoption is fastest. It is the peak in the second derivative of the logistic function and occurs when the third derivative equals zero.

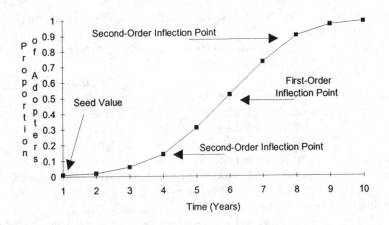

Figure 6.1. Cumulative adoption curve with inflection point and two second-order inflection points

Note: The inflection point occurs where the cumulative function is increasing most rapidly, the two second-order inflection points occur where the first derivative of the cumulative function is increasing and decreasing greatest. Data are from Ryan and Gross (1943) and represent the cumulative proportion of adopters of hybrid corn seed among farmers in two Iowa communities.

On a typical logistic diffusion curve, the first-order inflection point occurs at the average time of adoption, and the second-order inflection points occur at one standard deviation before and after the average time of adoption. Typically, the first-order inflection point for the logistic function occurs at 50% of adoption. However, the first-order inflection point may vary from 0% to 50%, depending on whether the diffusion process is external or mixed.

External influence diffusion occurs when an external force propels the diffusion of an innovation. The external force may be the mass media, a communication campaign, a structural change in the system, and so on. External influence diffusion often occurs when the mass media broadcast information about an event to the public. Awareness of the news spreads rapidly because the mass media reach many people simultaneously. For example, news of Eisenhower's heart attack in 1960 spread almost instantly, and the diffusion process was an external influence process (Deutschmann & Danielson, 1960). The curve for the external influence model of diffusion is depicted in Figure 6.2.

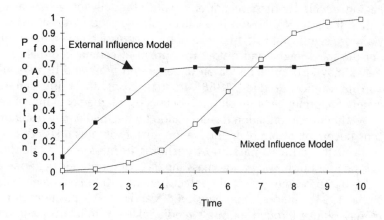

Figure 6.2. External and mixed influence models of the diffusion of innovations

Note: External influence data are from Deutschmann and Danielson (1960) and represent the proportion of individuals in Lansing, Michigan aware of then-president Eisenhower's stroke during the first day of its diffusion. The mixed influence data are from Ryan and Gross (1943) and represent the cumulative proportion of adopters of hybrid corn seed among farmers in two Iowa communities. The time scales are different, thus the data are not directly comparable.

Both models have different rates of diffusion, and hence a different critical mass point. The external influence model occurs when an external force propels diffusion and the rate of diffusion is very high. The mixed influence model occurs when both mass and interpersonal communication propel diffusion and the rate of diffusion is slower.

Mixed influence diffusion occurs when external influences such as the media, and internal forces such as interpersonal communication, are active in the spread of information. The mixed influence models (Barnett, 1988; Bass, 1969; Mahajan & Peterson, 1985; Valente, 1993) capture the influence of mass and interpersonal communication simultaneously. Mixed influence models occur most commonly in the spread of opinions or attitudes about some topic because both mass media and interpersonal influence play a persuasion role (also depicted in Figure 6.2).

If diffusion is a function of external influences, then all members of a social system are almost simultaneously aware of the news or innovation. The point on the curve at which the increase in the number of new adopters is greatest occurs at the first time period. The critical mass in such instances is at the start of the diffusion process. For example, news about a crisis such as a war or a natural disaster reported by the mass media is widely and rapidly disseminated. In such cases, the critical mass is reached as soon as the diffusion process begins.[3]

However, if diffusion is a mixed influence process, one in which contagion occurs by mass media and word-of-mouth interpersonal contact, then the rate of diffusion is relatively slower, and personal networks play a more significant role.[4] For example, a repressive government might censor the mass media and restrict the spread of certain information, yet the news may also circulate via an underground press and by person-to-person interaction (Inkeles, 1968). In such cases, the critical mass is extremely important because diffusion occurs by interpersonal influence.

Although information dissemination by the media may result in all persons becoming aware of an innovation, that awareness does not negate the role of the critical mass and thresholds in mass media situations. People hear about news via the mass media, but form their opinions and attitudes based on interpersonal contact (Valente, Kim, Lettenmeir, Glass, & Dibba, 1994). Although the diffusion of candidate X's position on recycling may diffuse through the mass media (external influence), the diffusion of a positive or negative attitude about candidate X's position on recycling may diffuse in a mixed process.

---

[3]Of course, it may be that a "critical mass" never occurs—everyone has access to the same information and is just as active in its diffusion, therefore, no group is responsible for creating a critical mass. This is likely to be true in many instances of the diffusion of information via the mass media.

[4]An exception occurs for spectacular news events that spread rapidly by word of mouth, such as an assassination (Greenberg, 1964).

Three Potential Critical Mass Points

The logistic function has an inflection point at 50% adoption and two second-order inflection points, one each at one standard deviation below and above the mean. For external influence models, diffusion has an early inflection point such as at 0%, 5%, or 10% adoption, and the increasing second-order inflection point may not exist because the function constantly decreases after the first-order inflection point.

The first-order inflection point may be the critical mass (Rice et al., 1990). The advantage to specification of a first-order inflection point as the critical mass is that this point represents the time period of greatest increase in the proportion of adopters. If a logistic function describes the diffusion process, then the inflection point usually occurs at about 50% adoption. At this point a majority have adopted, and the benefits of adopting are presumably perceived by most individuals as outweighing the costs.

However, earlier writings postulated that the critical mass occurred at the increasing second-order inflection point (Rogers, 1962). The second-order inflection point indicates that the number of new adopters is increasing most rapidly. This point occurs early in the diffusion process, when about 16% of the individuals have adopted, which is consistent with some people's intuitive feeling about the nature of the critical mass: It takes a few adopters to get the diffusion process going, yet that number would have to be less than 40% or 50% to qualify as the critical mass because 40% or 50% represents enough people that the outcome is assured.

A third possibility is that the critical mass is the seed value, the number of initial adopters (Griliches, 1957). The seed value also has intuitive appeal as a measure of the critical mass because it is most consistent with the definition in nuclear physics of having enough fissionable material "go critical." Critical mass is often discussed in terms of the number of individuals necessary to ensure the success of some collective action. Therefore, any diffusion process that reaches saturation must have a critical mass of individuals who most logically would be the first adopters.

Figure 6.3 indicates three potential critical mass points on a diffusion curve. As an innovation diffuses, the number of new adopters per time period increases. At the first-order inflection point the number of new adopters decreases, but the overall cumulative number of adopters continues to increase until saturation. Where then does the critical mass occur?

In the general case of diffusion depicted in Figure 6.3, any of these three potential critical mass points might be considered the critical mass depending on the innovation and the social structure in which diffusion occurs. For example, say that Figure 6.3 represents the diffusion of telephones in the United States. The critical mass might occur at 50% adoption because most people feel that it is necessary to have a telephone

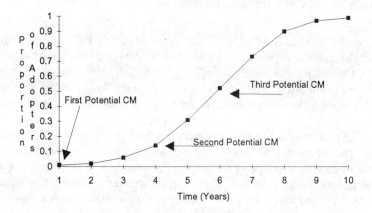

Figure 6.3. Three potential critical mass points

when a majority of people have one. However, if Figure 6.3 represents the diffusion of a new fertilizer among farmers, the critical mass may occur at the increasing second-order inflection point (at about 16% adoption) because the early adopters gain profits from their increased productivity, thus forcing other farmers to accelerate their adoption decisions for competitive reasons. Finally, if the S-curve in Figure 6.3 represents a collective action such as public support for building a new city park, the critical mass may occur almost immediately when one of the first people to adopt the idea contributes $40 million to the cost of the park project. Thus, the type of innovation influences the point of the critical mass.

STRUCTURAL MEASURES OF THE CRITICAL MASS

The social structure may also determine the point of the critical mass. If the most popular, resourceful, or influential individuals are the earliest to adopt an innovation, then critical mass will most likely occur earlier. Conversely, if the early adopters are social pariahs, outcasts, of low status, not resourceful, or not influential, critical mass is more likely to be delayed. So, the character of the early adopters affects the rate that others in the social system imitate their behavior and thus adopt the innovation.

These social structural properties constitute differences in resources or status that individuals possess which they may or may not contribute to the collective outcome. For example, in the diffusion of farming innovations, not all farmers are equal. Some have larger farms than others and hence bring a disproportionate amount of influence into the adoption process. Once larger farmers adopt the innovation they contribute proportionally more to achieving critical mass than when smaller farmers adopt.

Thus, for a given innovation in a given social system, reaching critical mass may occur when only a few farmers have adopted if these farmers own large farms. In a similar situation, in which the early adopters are farmers with small farms, it may take considerably longer for critical mass to be achieved. Note that the two cumulative adoption curves would be identical in the early stages, but as time passes the adoption curve for the early critical mass system would accelerate more rapidly.

A second manner in which individuals contribute disproportionately to achieving critical mass is captured by network analysis. The network structure indicates which individuals in the system act as opinion leaders and are thus more influential in the flow of influence. As discussed in Chapters 3 and 4, individuals with high centrality are connected in various ways to a greater number of others and therefore exert more influence.

If early adopters are individuals with high centrality scores, then they influence a greater number of other potential adopters than average members of the system. Therefore, diffusion is accelerated and critical mass is reached relatively earlier. If, on the other hand, early adoption is by individuals with low centrality scores, diffusion will take longer and critical mass occurs relatively later.

Moreover, other properties of the network, both for individuals and at the network level, influence the rate of diffusion and hence the critical mass. For example, network density was shown to be related to the speed of diffusion. In a dense network, the average number of connections between individuals is high. Therefore, once a few members of the network adopt an innovation they can influence and inform others more quickly. Hence it takes fewer individuals to constitute a critical mass.

Centralized networks reach critical mass more quickly if the early adopters are the central individuals. If the early adopters in a centralized network are on the periphery, the time it takes to reach critical mass is proportionate to the distance these early adopters are to the central nodes. The effect of central versus peripheral early adopters in both centralized and decentralized networks is also dependent on the size of the network. Ceteris paribus, in larger networks the relative effect of early adopters being peripherals, is to delay achieving critical mass and to slow the rate of diffusion.

The presence of weak ties facilitates critical mass because it permits the innovation to be spread to otherwise unconnected subgroups. Size, centralization, and characteristics of early adopters may be immaterial in their effect on the critical mass if weak ties are not present in the network to insure that subgroups share information with one another. As mentioned earlier, weak ties act as bridges, and the speed with which an innovation spreads in one group has no effect on others unless some bridge exists for the innovation to spread.

It is important to realize that the critical mass occurs early in the diffusion process but does not manifest itself until at least the inflection point. This is because cumulative adoption curves for an innovation in two separate communities may be identical until an inflection point is reached at about 16% cumulative adoption. At 16%, a diffusion process that has reached the critical mass has a faster rate of growth, and hence the diffusion curve rises more steeply.

Figure 6.4 shows hypothetical examples of three diffusion curves. When critical mass is achieved earlier, the diffusion curve rises more steeply and the inflection point is reached sooner. When critical mass is achieved later, the diffusion curves rise more slowly and the inflection point is reached later.

Unfortunately, scholars and lay people use the term *critical mass* irrespective of the kind of diffusion curve—whether external or mixed influence—and the nature of the social structure. Future research should specify the shape of the diffusion curve,[5] determine inflection points, analyze the type of innovation, and specify the network characteristics of adopters (especially early adopters). The critical mass can then be determined from these various diffusion characteristics, especially the network characteristics of early adopters.

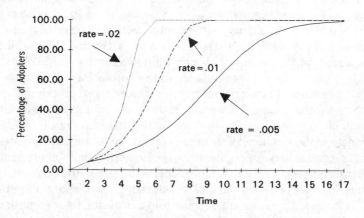

Figure 6.4. Three hypothetical diffusion curves

Note: When critical mass occurs early diffusion accelerates and the inflection point is reached earlier. In the second and third curves, critical mass is reached later or not all and so the inflection point occurs later.

---

[5]The diffusion curve is analagous to a production function.

FINDING CRITICAL MASS

As stated above the *critical mass* is the minimum number of participants needed to sustain a collective activity. The participants may be people, organizations, nations, or other units, or a structured subset of these units. The activity may be innovation diffusion, but it may also be collective action, consumer product market share, or public opinion, as well as such everyday activities as organizing a softball or a Thursday night poker game.

A key finding of Oliver, Marwell, and Teixeira (1985) was that the critical mass is composed of individuals who receive numerous nominations from others in the network. Indeed, the network models posited thus far indicate that centrality, both from relational and structural perspectives is important in the spread of innovations. In most diffusion situations there exists a pool of individuals who are central in the network who represent the potential critical mass. Once this pool of centrals adopts the innovation, and sufficient other network properties such as radiality, density, and weak ties are present, the critical mass occurs.

Thus, the *critical mass* exists when high centrality individuals are early adopters. The critical mass does not exist when high centrality individuals are late adopters or low centrality individuals are early adopters. To be sure, other network characteristics are important for determining the critical mass and the rate of the diffusion. For example, differentiation in the network and the existence of numerous subgroups slows diffusion and impedes the critical mass. When a network is divided into many small groups with few connections between them, early adoption by centrals might not be sufficient to achieve critical mass. Differentiation in either relational or structural attributes impedes the development of a critical mass and thus slows the rate of adoption.

It is in the context of network differentiation and the critical mass that weak ties become important. In undifferentiated networks, those with few subgroups, critical mass occurs when early adopters have high centrality. For differentiated networks, critical mass occurs when early adopters have high centrality and a sufficient number of weak ties are present to insure rapid diffusion to other subgroups.

Critical Mass Indicators

There are two manifest indicators of the critical mass: (a) a high rate of diffusion, and (b) a high level of saturation. These two indicators represent a different characteristic of the diffusion curve, yet reflect the role of the critical mass in diffusion: Namely, accelerating its rate and extending its reach.

To demonstrate the relationship between the critical mass and its indicators, a critical mass score was constructed and correlated with these

indicators for the data. The critical mass score for a system is a combination of the time of adoption and the centrality score of the individuals. The
critical mass score should be high if early adopters have high centrality
and low if early adopters have low centrality. The most straightforward
manner to combine centrality and time of adoption is to multiply them.

The trouble with simply multiplying centrality and time of adoption is
that the product is correlated with rate of diffusion even if central members
delay adoption. That is, if the rate of diffusion is high, relatively more individuals are early adopters (i.e., adopt at early time periods). Therefore, this multi-
plication score would increase proportionally to the number of early adopters.

TESTING CRITICAL MASS DEFINITIONS

To test whether early adoption by centrals constitutes the critical mass it is
necessary to simultaneously control for the rate of adoption. In other words,
any data that show that early adoption by centrals is associated with more
rapid diffusion is biased by the fact that rapid diffusion itself creates more
early adopters, thus making it more likely that centrals will adopt early.

The rate of adoption was controlled for by multiplying a vector of
centrality scores by the vector of adopters for each time period and then
adding the scores together. The sum provides a cumulative centrality score
for each time period. This time period centrality score is then divided by
the number of adopters at that time period. This normalizes the time period centrality score so that it is relative to the number of people who adopted at each time period. Thus, we have a normalized adoption centrality
score for each time period.

For example, if six individuals adopted at time period five, their
centrality scores are summed, then divided by six, which is the normalized
centrality for time period five. The normalized centrality scores for each
time period are progressively summed to give a cumulative centrality
adoption index for the time periods: 3 for medical doctors, 10 for Brazilian
farmers, and 6 for Korean family planning.[6]

Five critical mass indices were created with this procedure: (a)
nominations received, (b) centrality degree, (c) centrality closeness, (d)
centrality betweenness, and (e) radiality. The critical mass indices for each
network were rank ordered within each study so that those networks with
the highest critical mass index received lower ranks. For example, the
Korean family planning village number 22 received critical mass rank
indices of 5, 12, 6, 7, and 4, respectively.

Similarly, the villages were rank ordered within studies based on
their relative rate of adoption and saturation level such that the communi-

---

[6]These time periods were chosen so that cumulative adoption was about 15%.

ties with fastest diffusion and greatest saturation received the lowest number. Spearman rank order correlations were then computed to determine if early adoption by the five measures above were associated with faster diffusion or more extensive spread.

Critical mass indices based on nominations received and centrality degree were not associated with rate of diffusion or prevalence in either the Brazilian farmers or Korean women studies. Critical mass closeness was associated with diffusion prevalence in the Korean study only. Critical mass radiality was associated with diffusion rate in the Korean study only. Critical mass betweenness was associated with prevalence in the Brazilian study and both prevalence and rate in the Korean study (see Table 6.1).

The positive Spearman rank order correlation between critical mass betweenness and rate and prevalence of diffusion indicates that the critical mass is a function of relatively early adoption by individuals high in centrality betweenness. Early adoption by betweenness centrals provides more linkages in the network flow, thus facilitating information and influence in the network about the innovation. Betweenness centrals provide the links between groups and pockets in the network, thus shortening the distance between adopters and potential adopters. Betweenness centrals provide more pathways for the innovation to flow through the network.

Thus, the potential critical mass of adopters in a network consists of those individuals who have high betweenness centrality. More rapid diffusion occurs when betweenness centrals adopt early, and the diffusion is

Table 6.1. Spearman Rank Order Correlations Between Five Critical Mass Indices and Diffusion Prevalence and Diffusion Rate for the Brazilian Farmers and Korean Family Planning Studies.

Critical Mass Indices	Diffusion Indicators	
	Prevalence	Rate
Brazilian Farmers (N=10):		
Nominations Received	.23	-.56
Centrality - degree	.42	-.52
Centrality - closeness	.46	-.48
Centrality - betweenness	.66*	-.39
GRII	.64*	-.39
Korean Family Planning (N=25):		
Number Received	.15	.25
Centrality - degree	.25	.31
Centrality - closeness	.35*	.44*
Centrality - betweenness	.42*	.50**
GRII	.27	.47*

*$p < .05$; **$p < .01$

more likely to reach a greater percentage of individuals in the network. Note that this result is consistent with the weak tie theory which dictates that diffusion should occur more rapidly with the presence of weak ties because betweenness centrals provide weak ties between network subgroups.

One important implication of this result is that campaigns dedicated to achieving rapid diffusion of some product or idea should target betweenness centrals in order to promote more rapid and extensive spread. Opinion leaders have been targeted by campaigns to accelerate diffusion for this purpose. However, opinion leaders are often defined as those individuals who receive numerous nominations, that is, have a lot of ties in the network. If operationalized as such, these individuals may be local leaders only. In other words, they may have numerous ties, but those ties may be restricted to a group of individuals who only represent a subset of the whole network, even if that subset is a majority.

Lacking betweenness, such a local leader may not provide an effective bridge between disparate subgroups. Betweenness individuals link these groups, and although they may not have the greatest number of ties, their ties are sufficiently important to act as bridges between various groups and thus accelerate diffusion and insure that it reaches a larger majority.

SUMMARY

This chapter opened with a brief discussion of the uses of the critical mass. Three inflection point measures of the critical mass were presented: (a) the seed value (number of initial adopters), (b) the second-order inflection point, 16% adoption, and (c) the first-order inflection point, about 50% adoption. Each measure represents a different conceptualization of the critical mass and may be appropriate for different innovations. Further discussion of the critical mass focused on social structure properties such as wealth and network position as influences on the critical mass.

The critical mass was discussed in terms of centrality and, in particular, that central members of a network represent the potential critical mass in a social system. Should central members delay adoption, critical mass is not likely. However, early adoption by centrals represents a necessary but not sufficient condition because the early adoption by central members results in critical mass in undifferentiated networks, but is dependent on the presence of weak ties in differentiated networks.

Finally, we presented a critical mass score that multiplied centrality scores by time of adoption. The critical mass score was highly correlated with the two manifest indicators of the critical mass (rate of diffusion and saturation level). The positive correlations indicate that the critical mass accelerates diffusion, and the critical mass score provides a technique for determining the existence of a critical mass.

7

Empirical Analyses of Threshold Models*

This chapter presents empirical analysis of social network models of diffusion with the major datasets reviewed in Chapter 1. The models combine thresholds and the critical mass into a general diffusion network model that can be tested against empirical data to reveal aspects of network influence in the diffusion of innovations. The models tested in this chapter consider innovativeness relative to system and network simultaneously and show how these properties vary together and relate to external influences such as cosmopoliteness and media exposure.

The first section reviews micro- and macrolevels of analyses and discusses how the present models combine them. The next section presents empirical analyses of thresholds defined with respect to system and networks. The analysis shows that a dual classification of system and network thresholds reveals which individuals act as opinion leaders. These leaders act as agents of change and represent a critical mass of adopters.

Finally, the last section presents another adopter classification scheme based on network thresholds and a 50% point of the critical mass. This classification scheme attempts to combine micro and macro influences into one measure reducing the number of categories to only three. The assumptions for such a model may not always be met, and thus this may not be as widely applicable a model as a simple network threshold classification scheme.

---

*Portions of this chapter were presented at the Social Networks Sunbelt conferences of 1991 and 1992.

MICRO- AND MACROLEVELS OF ANALYSIS

In this section, the focus is on how exposure levels and thresholds affect the critical mass and how the critical mass affects thresholds. Does the exposure level distribution determine the point at which the critical mass is reached? Individuals with high exposure have early adoption, provided their threshold for adoption is sufficiently low. If individuals with high thresholds are the ones with high exposure, the rate of diffusion is slowed, yet if individuals with low thresholds receive high exposure, diffusion is accelerated and the critical mass is reached earlier in the diffusion process. So, exposure and thresholds affect the critical mass.

Does the critical mass affect thresholds? Prior to critical mass, adoption is risky, and only individuals with high exposure or low thresholds are likely to adopt an innovation. After the critical mass, adoption is not perceived as risky and therefore thresholds are more likely to be met, and less exposure is sufficient to persuade individuals to adopt. Risk influences adoption (Cancian, 1979); greater risk increases thresholds, and lower risk reduces thresholds.

Exposure determines when a critical mass is reached by structuring the flow of information about an innovation. If individuals with low thresholds receive high exposure, then the rate of diffusion accelerates, and critical mass is reached. When critical mass is reached, individuals lower their threshold and lower levels of exposure can provide enough incentive to adopt. There is a dynamic interaction between the individual-level threshold and the system-level critical mass point, and between the critical mass and thresholds.

Microlevel processes occur at the individual level of analysis. Personal efficacy, attitudes, and behavior are examples of variables involved in microlevel processes. Macrolevel processes occur at a system level of analysis. Societal efficacy, norms, and group behavior are examples of variables involved in macrolevel processes. Few research efforts have systematically analyzed the relationship between micro- and macrolevel processes.

Micro-macro Constructs and Patterns of Diffusion

Exposure levels and thresholds are microlevel constructs that characterize an individual's information environment. The critical mass is a macrolevel construct that characterizes a social system's diffusion pattern. Measuring network thresholds introduces the study of the influence of both the individual-level threshold and the system-level critical mass.

The critical mass is a system-level parameter, not an individual-level parameter. Exposure levels affect the critical mass, and the critical mass affects the efficacy of exposure, the threshold. The exposure and threshold distributions dictate the point at which a critical mass is reached. Once the critical mass is reached, more people's thresholds are met due to the increase in exposure.[1]

The relationship between external and mixed influence models, thresholds, and the critical mass defines the micro/macro diffusion process. The critical mass affects thresholds, and the exposure level distribution affects the point at which the system reaches critical mass. Those who have not adopted when critical mass is reached are more likely to have their thresholds met once the critical mass is reached because there are more adopters. They do so because the certainty of the outcome is assured, and after critical mass, it is cost-effective for an individual to engage in the behavior. The interaction between thresholds and the rise in exposure levels increases the rate of adoption.

Two processes occur during a dynamic micro-macro interaction of the threshold/critical mass (T/CM) theory. First, over time, as more and more individuals adopt, individuals are more likely to reach their threshold. Thus, exposure levels increase, and the exposure level distribution changes from being skewed right to skewed left. Second, over time, early adopters are able to experience the innovation and communicate that experience to others, thus allowing time for thresholds to be met and for threshold effects to occur.

One of the implications of the dynamic micro-macro hypothesis is that saturation can be avoided before the critical mass, but is increasingly difficult to avoid once the critical mass is reached. The consequence of threshold and critical mass effects is that individuals continually monitor their environment to gauge public opinion and behavior both on a mass and immediate level. People change their thresholds due to the opinion of others. If a critical mass of relevant others switches positions on an issue, then an individual is likely to change his or her opinion based on this shift. Allen's (1988) analysis of the French videotex system, Minitel, stated the case succinctly:

> It seems likely that individuals base their choice on what they expect the others to decide. Thus, the individual's effort to decide hinges upon "watching the group"—the other members in the community of actual/potential subscribers—to discern what the group choice may be. . . . The outcome for the group then turns literally upon everybody watching while being watched. Change, and finally critical mass for the group, floats it seems on shifting perceptions of what the group outcome may be. (p. 260)

---

[1]It may be that the critical mass actually decreases individual thresholds. However, the data do not exist to test such a model. Moreover, thresholds could not decrease below the network exposure level at that time.

A dynamic interplay occurs between the micro- and macrolevels of analysis. The model is more than an aggregation of individual behavior for the sake of making macrolevel predictions. A structural property of a system allows participants to sequentially influence the behavior of others. As more participants engage in an activity, they reciprocally influence earlier adopting participants by providing network externalities as social incentives to continue participating.

At the initial stage of diffusion only a few individuals adopt the innovation. Typically, these individuals adopt due to some influence that is external to the social system. These few adopters contribute to the exposure levels of the rest of the members. Thus, the exposure level distribution is skewed to the right. A *skewed right distribution* has a few values relatively much higher than the rest of the values in the distribution.

However, as the diffusion process progresses, more individuals adopt the innovation, and the exposure level distribution approaches a normal distribution. Toward the later stages of diffusion many more individuals adopt the innovation, and consequently the exposure level distribution becomes skewed to the left. A *skewed left distribution* has a few values relatively much lower than the rest of the values in the distribution.

An exposure level distribution that is skewed right indicates that some members of the social system have a high percentage of network partners who have adopted. At the early stages of diffusion, resistance is high, therefore only those members with high exposure levels are likely to adopt. As the diffusion process progresses, resistance to adoption decreases, and simultaneously, exposure levels increase. The interaction results in individuals meeting their threshold of adoption and adopting.

The rise in exposure levels accelerates the diffusion of innovations, which accelerates the point at which the system reaches critical mass. Thus, the microlevel measure of exposure influences the macrolevel of critical mass. The dynamic interplay works both ways: individual exposure levels influence the point at which critical mass is reached, and system-level critical mass affects the efficacy of exposure to influence adoption. In sum, we have a dynamic interplay between the microlevel threshold and the macrolevel critical mass. The next section reports the data from the three studies which show how the micro- and macrolevel measures relate to one another.

ADOPTER CATEGORIES

A major contribution to diffusion research has been the categorization of adopters based on innovativeness as measured by time of adoption. Adopters are classified as (a) early adopters, (b) early majority, (c) late majority, and (d) laggards (Beal & Bohlen, 1955; Rogers, 1983, pp. 245-247; Ryan & Gross, 1943, 1950).[2] *Early adopters* are individuals whose time of adoption is greater than one standard deviation earlier than the average time of adoption. The *early and late majorities* are individuals whose time of adoption is bounded by one standard deviation earlier and later than the average. Finally, *laggards* are those individuals who adopted later than one standard deviation from the mean.

The network threshold distribution may also be partitioned into adopter categories in the same manner described for time of adoption adopter categories. Specifically, *personal network very low thresholds* are individuals whose personal network threshold is greater than one standard deviation less than the average threshold. *Personal network low and high thresholds* are individuals whose network threshold is bounded by one standard deviation less than and greater than average. Finally, *personal network very high thresholds* are those individuals whose threshold is one standard deviation greater than average.

Adopter categories were created to compare early adopters with later adopters to determine differences in their social and personal characteristics, communication behavior, and opinion leadership. One of the primary research findings of diffusion research was that early adopters had more sources of external influence.

External Influence

Two possible external sources of influence on adoption of innovations are cosmopolitan[3] actions and communication media. Cosmopolitan actions and media consumption provide individuals with earlier awareness of an innovation (Becker, 1970; Fischer, 1978; Weimann, 1982) and freedom from system norms (Menzel, 1960), enabling them to be earlier adopters and proponents of an innovation. The thesis tested here is that the role of external influence on adoption of innovations is clarified when one considers thresholds relative to the social system and personal networks. Furthermore, this dual classification permits specification of how external and interpersonal influence flow through the system and govern the diffusion of innovations.

---

[2]Rogers's (1983) classification includes *innovators*, who are individuals who adopt extremely early. Innovators are interesting in that they are the very first to adopt, but here they are included with early adopters because they represent a small fraction of the sample.

[3]A *cosmopolite* is an individual who is oriented to the world outside of his or her local social system (Merton, 1968) and who relates his or her local social system to the larger environment by providing links to outside information (Davis, 1961; Gouldner, 1957, 1958).

Table 7.1 shows how individuals may be partitioned into adopter categories based on innovativeness relative to system and personal networks. The table cross classifies individuals by their threshold relative to the whole social system and their threshold relative to their network (however it is defined). This cross classification creates a 16 cell adopter classification scheme.

Table 7.2 shows the cell percentages for the adopter categories relative to the system and relative to personal networks for all three datasets. The first thing to notice about this table is that the two variables are associated with one another (χ^2, $p < .001$) for all three datasets. This is not surprising given that one's time of adoption is associated with the proportion of adopters in the social system, thus associated with the proportion in any individual's personal network (recall the correlations between network thresholds and system thresholds reported in Chapter 5).

Forty-three percent of the doctors in the medical innovation study were classified the same in both their social system and personal network thresholds. For the Brazilian farmers, 47% were classified the same; whereas 64% of the Korean women were classified the same. The proportion not classified similarly are in the off diagonal cells and represent individuals who are more innovative relative to the system than their network (upper triangle) or more innovative relative to their personal network than the system (lower triangle). For example, in row 1 column 2, 4.8% of the doctors are more innovative relative to the system because they adopted in the early adopter phase, yet had low thresholds to adoption.

Also of note, for the Brazilian farmers, all those in the laggard phase have either very low or high thresholds (row 11, columns 1 and 4). This is also true for the Korean women (row 12, columns 1 and 4) with the additional provision that all very high thresholds are nonadopters (rows 3, 6 and 9, column 4). These empty cells represent skewness in the data that

Table 7.1. Adopter Categories for Combined System and Network Thresholds.

EA/VLT	EA/LT	EA/HT	EA/VHT
EM/VLT	EM/LT	EM/HT	EM/VHT
LM/VLT	LM/LT	LM/HT	LM/VHT
LAG/VLT	LAG/LT	LAG/HT	LAG/VHT

Key:	EA: Early Adopters	EM: Early Majority
	LM: Late Majority	LAG: Laggards
	VLT: Very Low Threshold	LT: Low Threshold
	HT: High Threshold	VHT: Very High Threshold

Table 7.2. Proportions for Adopter Categories Based on Innovativeness Relative to Social System and Innovativeness Relative to Personal Networks.

		Personal Network: Direct Ties				
Doctors Farmers Women		Very Low Thresh.	Low Thresh.	High Thresh.	Very High Thresh	System Total
	Early	9.6	4.8	1.6	-	16.0
	Adopters	12.9	6.9	1.9	1.9	23.5
		12.7	8.0	2.6	-	23.3
S	Early	12.0	12.8	8.0	11.2	44.0
y	Majority	4.5	6.9	1.2	2.7	15.3
s		4.0	10.5	10.9	-	25.4
t						
e	Late	4.8	0.8	2.4	10.4	18.4
m	Majority	5.5	6.6	8.8	18.2	39.2
		2.3	5.2	8.1	-	35.7
	Laggard	1.6	.8	.8	18.4	21.6
		3.6	-	-	18.3	22.0
		3.1	-	-	32.6	35.7
Personal		28.0	19.2	12.8	40.0	100
Network		26.4	20.5	11.8	41.2	100
Total		22.2	23.7	21.6	32.6	100

Note: Variables in all three datasets are significantly associated with one another, χ^2, $p < .001$. Proportions in diagonal cells are classified the same as innovative relative to system and network.

arises from considerable proportions of nonadopters in the respective datasets: 22% for the Brazilian farmers, 32.6% for the Korean women. The reason for this skewness is that the respective innovations have not finished diffusing.

For readers more graphically inclined, the classification of the Brazilian farmers data by system and network thresholds is presented in Figure 7.1. The figure shows how uneven the system thresholds are in terms of the time dimension. It takes much longer for enough farmers to adopt to reach the first inflection point (approximately 15%) then it does to reach the midpoint of diffusion.

Table 7.3 reports the external influence scores for each of the 16 categories of adopters for the three datasets. The table shows how external influence scores vary for individuals who are innovative relative to the two dimensions. For example, doctors who are most innovative relative to the social system and relative to their network (row 1, column 1) subscribed to an average 5.17 journals. Farmers in this category made an average of 12.11 visits to the nearest large city in the past year, and Korean women scored 12.69 on the campaign exposure scale.

Doctors who were early adopters relative to the system and who had low thresholds subscribed to an average of 4.17 journals (row 4, column 2). Farmers in this category made an average of 7.83 visits to the nearest large city in the past year, and Korean women scored 15.06 on the campaign exposure scale in which high scores indicate high exposure.

Analysis of variance was conducted to test the association between the innovativeness variables and external influence. The ANOVA results were not consistent across datasets, indicating that external influence may have operated differently in the three studies. For example, doctors' journal subscriptions were not associated with either innovativeness dimension, whereas farmers' visits to the city were associated with both innovativeness dimensions and the interaction term (see Table 7.3).

Some important points need to be made about Table 7.3. First, external influence scores are almost always highest for individuals who are most innovative relative to the system and their personal network (very low threshold). These are the earliest adopters (innovators) who are the first to adopt the innovation. Their early adoption is associated with high external influence.

Second, the upper triangle scores are usually greater than their

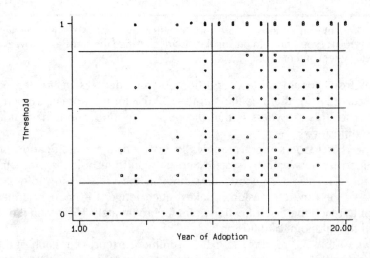

Figure 7.1. Network threshold by year of adoption for the Brazilian farmers data with classification level drawn in

respective lower triangle scores, indicating that external influence tends to make individuals innovative relative to the social system more than relative to their personal network.

Third, one would expect that within diffusion phases the external influence scores would be monotonic by network thresholds. In other words, if system and personal network influences acted serially then the scores would be greatest for early adopters relative to the system, next for early majority adopters, and so on, which is indeed the case. However, within each phase one would expect that very low thresholds would have the highest external influence score, followed by network low thresholds, followed by those with high thresholds, and finally those with very high thresholds. This is not the case. In fact, generally, the diagonal element is the largest or next largest external influence score. This indicates that individuals who are consistent in their innovativeness (in both macro- and microlevels) tend to experience the highest external influence in their adoption phase.

Table 7.3. External Influence (Journal Subscriptions, City Visits, Campaign Exposure) by System and Cohesion Network Thresholds.

		Personal Network: Direct Ties				
Journals[a] Visits[b] Campaign[c]		Very Low Thresh.	Low Thresh.	High Thresh.	Very High Thresh	System Total
	Early	5.17	4.17	4.50	-	4.80
	Adopters	12.11	7.83	2.54	3.08	9.35
S		12.69	15.06	13.66	-	13.62
y	Early	3.33	5.06	4.50	4.21	4.27
s	Majority	10.81	8.00	2.25	4.79	7.81
t		8.14	14.22	13.55	-	12.98
e	Late	3.83	8.00	4.00	4.00	4.13
m	Majority	4.16	3.80	4.92	3.88	4.14
		11.02	13.67	14.32	-	13.67
	Laggard	3.50	2.00	2.00	3.35	3.26
		1.96	-	-	6.78	5.98
		6.76	-	-	10.29	10.03
Personal		4.06	4.83	4.25	3.76	4.11
Network		8.84	6.58	4.27	5.19	6.33
Total		6.97	8.94	8.36	5.92	12.22

[a]ANOVA main and interaction term associations are nonsignificant.
[b]ANOVA main and interaction term associations are significant at $p < .05$.
[c]ANOVA main effects association is significant at $p < .001$ and interaction term is nonsignificant.

Fourth, the laggards, those who never adopt or adopt late, can be partitioned into isolates and very high thresholds. Those in the laggard phase who are classified as very low thresholds have still not received exposure to the innovation from their network and (according to Table 7.3) are not being exposed to the innovation through external influence. It is unclear whether these isolates will ever adopt because there seems to be no mechanism for them to learn about the innovation.

On the other hand, there are laggards who have very high network thresholds, hear about the innovation, but are still not persuaded to adopt. Thus, we have partitioned nonadopters into those who did not adopt, perhaps because they did not hear about the innovation (rows 10-12, column 1), and those who did not adopt, perhaps due to resistance (rows 10-12, column 4).

External influence scores by innovativeness relative to system and structural equivalence were also computed. Space limitations prohibit repeating all the tables for the SE network. The overall pattern of results is less interpretable for the structural equivalence thresholds compared to the cohesion results. This is mainly because the interaction term is not significant for any of the external influence results. Consequently, the external influence scores do not cluster along the diagonal and do not seem to vary in any consistent manner. It is important to note, however, that the SE threshold scores are different from those reported for the cohesion thresholds. (It is also possible to create a table in which cohesion and structural equivalence thresholds make up the row and column headings, and those cases that fall in the diagonal make up respondents who are consistent in their network thresholds.)

As mentioned above, although external influences are generally responsible for making individuals aware of innovations, it is often interpersonal influence with friends and neighbors that leads to actual adoption. The long-standing theory of diffusion has been that the media, salesmen, campaigns, targeted literature, and other factors make individuals aware of innovations, but interpersonal persuasion is necessary to convince individuals to adopt (Rogers, 1983; Ryan & Gross, 1943). Thus, the two-step flow hypothesis was created (Katz, 1957; Weimann, 1982), which stated that the media inform opinion leaders who, in a second step, influence opinion followers.

Social network thresholds permit specification of this two-step flow by postulating that opinion leaders are those with lower thresholds who influence those with higher thresholds to adopt. If this is true, innovativeness relative to one's personal network should be associated with opinion leadership. *Opinion leadership* is measured by the number of network nominations received (Rogers & Cartano, 1962). In fact, the pattern of network nominations received for the 16 categories of adopters indicates the flow of interpersonal influence.

Table 7.4 shows the average number of nominations received for the 16 categories for the three datasets. First, notice that the highest scores generally occur along the diagonal. This indicates that individuals who adopt when their system and network level exposure are about the same are more likely to be opinion leaders. Thus, opinion leaders are behaving in a normative fashion by having consistency in their system and personal network thresholds.

For individuals who adopt early relative to the system, it is normative for them to adopt with very low network thresholds, and these individuals are more likely to be opinion leaders. For example, doctors who adopt early relative to both system and network (row 1, column 1) receive an average of 3.08 nominations. Early adopter doctors (system-level) who adopt with low network thresholds (row 1, column 2) receive an average of 2.0 network nominations, compared to early adopter doctors who adopt with high network thresholds who receive only 1.5 network nominations.

Table 7.4. Opinion Leadership Scores (Number of Network Nominations Received) by System and Cohesion Network Categories.

Doctors[a] Farmers[b] Women[c]		Personal Network: Direct Ties				
		Very Low Thresh.	Low Thresh.	High Thresh.	Very High Thresh	System Total
	Early	3.08	2.00	1.50	-	2.60
	Adopters	3.07	1.77	4.38	3.23	2.80
S		5.47	5.24	5.04	-	5.34
y	Early	1.27	4.31	3.50	2.29	2.82
s	Majority	3.45	3.94	8.00	2.47	3.84
t		3.05	4.86	4.69	-	4.50
e	Late	1.00	2.00	5.33	2.23	2.30
m	Majority	2.84	2.91	2.87	2.71	2.80
		2.38	3.69	3.91	-	3.61
	Laggard	0.50	0.00	2.00	1.35	1.26
		0.40	-	-	1.48	1.30
		1.36	-	-	3.15	2.99
Personal		1.80	3.46	3.50	1.84	2.35
Network		2.72	2.87	3.61	2.17	2.63
Total		4.13	4.73	4.44	3.15	4.02

[a]ANOVA diffusion phase significant at $p < .05$.
[b]ANOVA network threshold significant at $p < .01$.
[c]ANOVA both main effects significant at $p < .001$.

For early majority doctors, row 4, those who adopt with low network thresholds have the highest number of network nominations received, 4.31.

Individuals who exhibit consistency in their thresholds are appropriate role models and near peers whose behavior may be imitated. Individuals who are more innovative relative to their network for that phase of diffusion are generally not appropriate role models for others at that stage. These individuals deviate from the norm for that stage of diffusion and hence cannot act as role models for others.

Second, notice that the pattern of nominations received is different for the three datasets. The opinion leadership scores increase along the diagonal for the medical innovation data, but show several inconsistencies for the Brazilian farmers, and decrease along the diagonal for the Korean women. This may indicate that the flow of interpersonal influence was different in the three studies.

As Coleman et al. (1966) showed, innovation in the medical community was usually associated with integration. In other words, diffusion occurred via contagion, like a snowball process, in which doctors who were connected to each other influenced one another through their ties within the social system. This is generally true, and within each diffusion phase, doctors who are consistent relative to the system and their personal network are the opinion leaders.

However, the earliest adopters relative to the system may be oriented to the larger medical community, perhaps in Chicago or New York (as also evidenced by their journal subscriptions). Consequently, these early adopter doctors do not receive the most nominations within the system, and their opinion leadership scores are depressed by their external system contact.[4]

In contrast, the Brazilian farmers data contain inconsistencies in the distribution of opinion leadership scores. Within some diffusion phases, opinion leadership scores are highest for farmers in off-diagonal cells. For example, in the early adopter phase, farmers who adopted with high network thresholds had the greatest number of nominations received (this may be a result of the small percentage who fall into this category; see Table 7.2). Consequently, interpersonal influence may not have flowed through the Brazilian farmer networks in a discernable pattern.

For the Korean women data, opinion leadership seemed to follow the classic diffusion model. That is, opinion leader scores are highest along the diagonal, indicating that individuals who were consistent in their

---

[4]A second reason for the lower opinion leadership scores for the earlier adopters is the inherent conservatism in the medical community. As mentioned throughout the Coleman et al. (1966) and Burt (1987) analyses, doctors must turn to others for advice and reassurance concerning the adoption of new therapies. The risk and uncertainty associated with innovation forces doctors to wait until a sufficient number of other doctors in the system adopt.

thresholds were more likely to be opinion leaders. Moreover, network nominations received are highest for women who adopted earliest. That is, early adopters relative to system and personal network received the most nominations for that phase and received the most nominations overall (5.47 nominations, row 3, column 1). Women who adopted early majority with low network thresholds received the second highest opinion leadership scores (4.86 nominations), and late majority women received the third most, 3.91.

Opinion leadership by earlier adopters indicates that the flow of interpersonal influence was perhaps contained within the social system of Korean women. That is, the early adopters of family planning became opinion leaders in their communities and may have disseminated information and influence about family planning to other members of their village. The later adopters turned to these earlier adopters, perhaps to get more information or reassurance about modern family planning methods. These later adopters would then adopt, but the earliest adopters would still remain the opinion leaders in the village.

It may be that innovativeness contributed to the opinion leadership of the Korean women. The Korean women who adopted early became opinion leaders, perhaps in part due to their early adoption of innovations. In contrast, the medical doctors' opinion structure did not change as a result of adoption behavior. To be sure, doctors who had low network thresholds were considered opinion leaders within their phase of diffusion. But early adoption of tetracycline perhaps did not increase the likelihood a doctor would be considered an opinion leader in the community.

Why are these two opinion processes different? In other words, why is innovativeness associated with opinion leadership for Korean women and not for Illinois medical doctors? The medical community is an extremely hierarchical social system in which standards of perceived excellence such as medical school attended, sophistication of clients, and so on, are clearly known. In contrast, rural Korean women in the 1960s probably based social status, and hence opinion leadership, on degree of modernity, wealth, education, and other factors that are associated with adoption of modern family planning practices.

In sum, it seems that the diffusion of innovations in these three datasets followed three different patterns and perhaps were the result of three different influence processes. For the medical innovation data, doctors connected to the greater medical community in Chicago or New York may have been the first to adopt and became opinion leaders for their phase of diffusion. Subsequent adoption was probably based on opinion leadership within phases. Thus, the medical innovation data support the two-step flow model in which external influence leads to opinion leadership within phases of diffusion, but not across phases.

For Brazilian farmers, cosmopolitan contact as measured by visits to the nearest city had the strongest influence on adoption of hybrid corn, and interpersonal influence seemed to be less structured. Thus, for Brazilian farmers, it may be that cosmopoliteness was associated with earlier adoption but not associated with opinion leadership.

For Korean women, the classic two-step flow model seemed to operate in which consistency between system and network thresholds was associated with opinion leadership. This opinion leadership was also associated with external influence from the media campaign. Finally, the earliest adopters were considered opinion leaders for the entire village, not just individuals who adopted in the same stage.

The dual classification of adopters according to their innovativeness relative to system and personal network provided insight into the influence flow process in the datasets. Considerably more analysis could be conducted to determine the characteristics of individuals who have low network thresholds with high system thresholds, or vice versa. Moreover, future studies can investigate the similarities or differences that emerge in these tables when the network threshold is created on different properties such as structural equivalence, centrality, prominence, and so on.

The central point is that thresholds can be created relative to network properties as well as relative to overall system behavior. Adopter categories can be created from the threshold distributions and cross classified with time of adoption to understand the diffusion process. The next section presents a combined threshold/critical mass classification.

A THRESHOLD/CRITICAL MASS (T/CM) MODEL

A threshold/critical mass (T/CM) model is introduced to provide an alternative to the dual classification scheme presented earlier. This T/CM model requires a threshold measure and a determination of the critical mass. The critical mass (see Chapter 6) represents a complex interaction of individual adoption behavior and network properties. The earliness of the critical mass's adoption behavior accelerates the rate of diffusion such that the cumulative adoption curve rises more steeply. Accelerated diffusion curves have lower inflection points, and thus reach the point when 50% of the population has adopted earlier. So the critical mass directly affects the location of inflection points. Because the critical mass determines the rate of diffusion, hence, the inflection point, the inflection point can act as a proxy representation of the critical mass during diffusion.

The two components of the threshold/critical mass model—a personal network threshold computed from exposure and the critical mass operationalized as the 50% adoption point—have been introduced. What remains is the description of a theoretical curve that enables adopter classification based on low and high thresholds (see Figure 7.2). Recall that thresholds are measured by exposure which increases over time. Therefore, classification of adopters based on thresholds may be time dependent and relative to exposure. That is, an 80% exposure would be extremely high at the second or third time period of diffusion because few people in the system have adopted and so few networks would have 80% adopters. However, toward the end of diffusion, 80% exposure is below average since many personal networks are filled with adopters.

At the start of diffusion, risk to adoption and uncertainty about the innovation are high because no one in the social system has adopted. A few individuals may adopt due to media or cosmopolitan influences, thus creating some personal network exposure and a low average system-level exposure. If an individual adopts at this time period (or the next one) with an exposure somewhat greater than average exposure, he or she still has a low threshold because the behavior is very risky and uncertain.

In other words, early in the diffusion process, individuals classified as low threshold adopters can have greater than average exposure, and, in fact, first time period adopters are categorized as having low thresholds if their threshold is less than one standard deviation above the average exposure. Those individuals with thresholds greater than one standard deviation above average exposure have high thresholds. The choice of a one standard deviation above average exposure cut-off value represents the additional

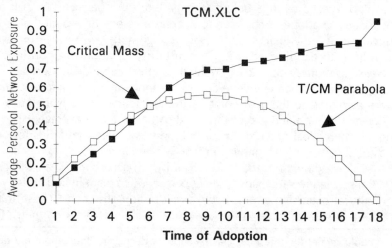

Figure 7.2. Average exposure for the whole system increases during diffusion

Note: The theoretical threshold/critical mass curve represents the values that distinguish high- and low-threshold adopters. The parabola is constructed from the points (1, .12), (6, .5), and (18, 0), which yields the equation $-.0069x^2 + .1245x + .0025$.

exposure needed to overcome the risk and uncertainty associated with early adoption (one could choose two standard deviations if desired).

During the early stage of diffusion, the struggle for conformity and the competing pressures of adopter/nonadopter interaction increase the uncertainty and risk to adoption (Cancian, 1979; Moscovici, 1976). The classification curve increases slightly and so does average exposure. As more individuals adopt over time, risk to adoption decreases marginally (Cancian, 1979, p. 63) and average exposure continues to increase because individuals continue to adopt. Consequently, because risk is reduced, the classification curve decreases relative to average exposure (converging toward average exposure), yet continues to increase absolutely.

The inflection point indicates the system level at which the risk and uncertainty about the outcome of diffusion have decreased to a level such that average exposure is sufficient for adoption. At the inflection point, high thresholds are thresholds that are greater than average exposure, and low thresholds are thresholds that are less than average exposure. The inflection point represents the time when individuals have equal influences for adoption/nonadoption from the social system. If exposure is less than 50%, adoption by the individual represents counter-normative behavior, and thus the individual is classified as a low threshold adopter. If exposure is greater than 50% at adoption by the individual, this represents normative behavior, and thus the individual is classified as a high threshold adopter.

After the inflection point, the theoretical curve distinguishing low and high thresholds dips below average exposure because the risk and uncertainty to adoption continue to decrease. At one time period after the critical mass, individuals with thresholds slightly below average exposure have high thresholds. Risk and uncertainty of adoption continue to decrease as more people adopt so the theoretical curve decreases.

Finally, when everyone adopts the innovation, risk and uncertainty are zero, and so the final point for the theoretical curve is the last time period of diffusion and a zero threshold. An example of average exposure and the theoretical curve distinguishing low and high thresholds for doctors adopting a medical innovation is shown in Figure 7.2.[5]

For example, in the diffusion of hybrid seed corn (Ryan & Gross, 1943) a few farmers (perhaps 5%) are persuaded to plant hybrid corn by an agricultural extension agent or by a media advertisement. These initial adopters then contribute to the exposure of their network partners. This

[5]We could model the threshold classification as decreasing throughout the diffusion process. That is, risk and uncertainty decrease at a constant rate during diffusion. The threshold curve in Figure 7.2 would be a diagonal line extending from the upper left hand corner of the graph (1, 1) to the lower right hand corner (18, 0). This analysis was performed, and the adopter categories produced were highly correlated with adopter categories constructed on the basis of time of adoption and thus did not offer new insights into the diffusion process.

influence gives some farmers exposure levels of 10% or 20%, and average exposure level in the community of between 0% and 20%. During the next few years, low threshold farmers adopt before many of their network partners adopt because they are exposed to the hybrid seed via mass media or cosmopolitan contacts with other communities. High threshold farmers adopt hybrid corn only after many of their network partners have adopted.

After 50% of the farmers in the community adopt hybrid corn, individuals have overwhelming evidence from the other members of their social system that hybrid corn is advantageous, and they should lower their threshold for adoption. If their threshold still remains higher than average exposure, then they are still resistant to the innovation. That is, the system-level evidence clearly shows that hybrid corn is advantageous, yet the individual resists in spite of personal network exposure to the innovation. The classification of high threshold adopters decreases from 50% to 40% and finally to zero after everyone has adopted.

This theoretical threshold/critical mass relationship can be approximated by a parabola of the form:

$$y(t) = at^2 + bt + c$$

in which a, b, and c are coefficients and t represents time. The equation for a parabola has three unknowns; therefore, three data points are necessary to solve the equation. The data points consist of the x-axis time of adoption and the y-axis threshold (time, threshold). The x coordinate for the first data point is the first time period of study (time period one), thus x=1. The y coordinate for the first data point is a high threshold, defined as one standard deviation above average exposure.

For the medical innovation data, one standard deviation above average exposure at time period one is .12, thus the first data point for the parabola is (1, .12). The second point is the critical mass threshold of 50% which occurs at time period six. Thus the second data point is (6, .5). The third data point is based on the assumption that there is no resistance to the innovation after everyone has adopted (time period 18), thus it equals (18, 0). The parabolic function derived from these data points is $-.0069t^2 + .1245t + .0025$. The T/CM classification categorizes adopters according to their threshold and the threshold/critical mass parabola. The T/CM adopter categories are: zero, low, and high threshold.

Empirical Analysis of T/CM Model

Figure 7.3 graphs thresholds and the adopter classification curve for the Brazilian farmers data. The threshold/critical mass model creates three categories of doctors: (a) zero T/CM (arrayed along the horizontal axis), (b) low T/CM (below the T/CM parabola), and (c) high T/CM (above the T/CM

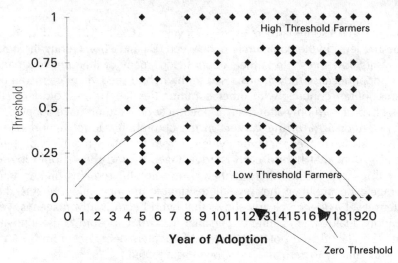

Figure 7.3. The distribution thresholds in the T/CM model for the diffusion of hybrid seed corn among Brazilian farmers

Note: Data are from Herzog, Stanfield, Whiting, and Svenning (1968).

parabola). High T/CM doctors required more interpersonal influences from adopters to adopt than did zero T/CM or low T/CM doctors.

The T/CM adopter classification also permits specification of who influenced whom during the diffusion process. High T/CM doctors were influenced by other doctors in the social system. Low and zero T/CM doctors were less dependent on their personal network for adoption influence and may have been influenced by sources outside of the social system. Again, two possible external sources of influence are cosmopolitan actions (such as out-of-town visits) and the mass media.

T/CM categories were created for both cohesion (direct ties) and structural equivalence personal networks. Space limitations again prohibit presenting the results of both cohesion and SE classifications. The results for the cohesion and SE T/CM models are similar (i.e., the pattern of scores on the external influence variables are the same) and thus do not warrant repeating.

The results that follow indicate that low T/CM individuals have greater exposure, through cosmopoliteness and media use, to the innovation and thus are more willing to adopt the innovation before many others in their personal network. Results for the SE T/CM model are presented below, and they are the same as those obtained for the cohesion model. As a reminder, the SE influences are from the individual's immediate network, a small radius of social influence analogous to the cohesion model presented earlier in this chapter.

Table 7.5 reports the number of medical journals subscribed to for each T/CM adopter category. Low T/CM doctors subscribed to more journals, and thus were more cosmopolitan, than either zero or high T/CM doctors. Low T/CM adopters were more likely to be women's club members than zero or high T/CM adopters, and they scored highest on the media campaign exposure scale (see Table 7.5). Thus, low T/CM women received information about family planning from sources external to their village.

Although low T/CM adopters had the highest external contact for the doctors and Korean women, zero SE T/CM farmers scored highest on number of visits to the nearest large city.[6] This indicates that these external influences may be associated with very early adoption relative to structurally equivalent others. In other words, external influences for the Brazilian farmers resulted in farmers being more innovative than other farmers of the same status. So, low SE T/CM doctors and Korean women and zero SE T/CM farmers have the highest external influence scores.

A second indicator of external contact is the use of media for agricultural information, which was measured with a scale of six media use questions (see Appendix A). The results (see Table 7.5) show again that zero T/CM farmers had higher media use scores than low or high T/CM farmers. Thus, zero SE T/CM farmers made greater use of media sources in their adoption behavior.

In general, then, it seems that low T/CM adopters have the highest level of external system contact for the medical doctors and Korean

Table 7.5. Scores on Cosmopoliteness Extra-system Contact, Media Subscribership, and Media Exposure For Structural Equivalence Threshold/Critical Mass (T/CM) Adopter Categories.

	Zero T/CM	Low T/CM	High T/CM	Sig.
Illinois Doctors ($N = 125$)	($N = 11$)	($N = 44$)	($N = 70$)	
Journal Subscriptions	3.18	**4.41**	4.07	p = ns
Brazilian Farmers ($N = 692$)	($N = 41$)	($N = 250$)	($N = 401$)	
Visits to City	**9.10**	7.52	5.31	$p < .05$
Media Sources	**3.80**	3.11	2.56	$p < .001$
Korean Rural Women				
($N = 1047$)	($N = 64$)	($N = 302$)	($N = 680$)	
Women's Club Member	43.5%	**55.4%**	40.2%	$p < .001$
Media Campaign Exposure	10.72	**13.30**	11.86	$p < .01$

[6]This is also true for the cohesion T/CM adopters. That is, zero cohesion T/CM adopters also have the highest number of city visits.

women, and zero T/CM adopters have the highest level of external contact for the Brazilian farmers. Do low T/CM adopters also have the highest level of network activity? Table 7.6 reports the number of network nominations received for the T/CM categories in the three datasets. Low T/CM adopters receive the most network nominations in the medical doctors and Korean women studies, but zero T/CM farmers receive the most nominations in the Brazilian dataset.

As Table 7.6 shows, low T/CM doctors and women received more nominations than zero or high T/CM doctors and women. Zero T/CM farmers received the most network nominations in the Brazilian farmers dataset and were also more likely to be nominated as agricultural advisors to other farmers. Thus, it seems that the T/CM model identified opinion leaders as those in the low T/CM category for doctors and Korean women, and those in the zero T/CM category for the Brazilian farmers.

Note how these results compare to those presented earlier in the dual classification of system and network thresholds. That analysis showed that the pattern of external influence and opinion leadership scores in the Brazilian data were hard to interpret and concluded that perhaps external influence did not influence adoption and diffusion. Here when combining threshold and critical mass we conclude that zero T/CM is associated with greater external influence. It seems that by focusing on the threshold value alone, with less concern for the system-level information, it has helped reveal that external influence did influence adoption behavior for the Brazilian farmers data.

The trouble with the T/CM model is that it does not report the overlap between low T/CM adopters and time of adoption. Consequently,

Table 7.6. Opinion Leadership Scores (Number of Nominations Received) for Structural Equivalence Threshold/Critical Mass (T/CM) Adopter Categories.

	Zero T/CM	Low T/CM	High T/CM	Sig.
Illinois Doctors ($N = 125$)	($N = 11$)	($N = 44$)	($N = 70$)	
Received	1.7	2.7	2.2	p = ns
Brazilian Farmers ($N = 692$)	($N = 41$)	($N = 250$)	($N = 401$)	
Received	4.2	2.9	2.3	$p < .05$
Agricultural Advisor	2.6	1.8	.9	$p < .001$
Korean Rural Women				
($N = 1047$)	($N = 64$)	($N = 302$)	($N = 681$)	
Received	2.8	4.5	3.9	$p < .01$

associations between T/CM categories and external influence (or other) variables may be synonymous with results that would be obtained if one examined thresholds with respect to the system alone. Thus, the disadvantage of the T/CM model is that it does not completely account for both levels of analysis.

In summary, low T/CM doctors gained exposure to the innovation due to their cosmopoliteness, and then, due to their greater social activity, they influenced many other doctors. Low T/CM doctors acted as leaders in the diffusion of tetracycline. High T/CM doctors were followers who waited until a high proportion of their network adopted before adopting. Zero T/CM doctors were social isolates not connected to the flow of influence. The same can also be said for low T/CM Korean women who acted as leaders in the diffusion of modern family planning practices. For Brazilian farmers, zero T/CM farmers acted as leaders in the diffusion hybrid corn adoption.

SUMMARY

This chapter presented data to show how network threshold adopter categories relate to system thresholds. Then tables were presented in which the external influence scores for the 16 possible threshold combinations were demonstrated. The results indicated that individuals who are consistent in their system and network thresholds generally act as opinion leaders.

It seems that the diffusion of innovations in these three datasets followed three different patterns and perhaps were the result of three different influence processes. For the medical innovation data, doctors connected to the greater medical community in Chicago or New York may have been the first to adopt and became opinion leaders for their phase of diffusion. Subsequent adoption was probably based on opinion leadership within phases. Thus, the medical innovation data support the two-step flow model in which external influence leads to opinion leadership within phases of diffusion, but not across phases.

For Brazilian farmers, cosmopolitan contact as measured by visits to the nearest city had the strongest influence on adoption of hybrid corn, and interpersonal influence seemed to be less structured. Thus, for Brazilian farmers, it may be that cosmopoliteness was associated with earlier adoption, but was not associated with opinion leadership.

For Korean women, the classic two-step flow model seemed to operate in which consistency between system and network thresholds was associated with opinion leadership. This opinion leadership was also associated with external influence from the media campaign. Finally, the earliest adopters were considered opinion leaders for the entire village, not just individuals who adopted in the same stage.

The dual classification of adopters according to their innovative-ness relative to system and personal network provided insight into the influence flow process in the datasets. Considerably more analysis could be conducted to determine the characteristics of individuals who have low network thresholds with high system thresholds, or vice versa. Moreover, future studies can investigate the similarities or differences that emerge in these tables when the network threshold is created on different properties such as structural equivalence, centrality, prominence, and so on.

The central point of this chapter is that thresholds can be created relative to network properties as well as relative to overall system behav-ior. Adopter categories can be created from the threshold distributions and cross classified with time of adoption to understand the diffusion process. Figure 7.4 presents a sociogram of cohesion network thresholds in which arrows between individuals represent direct communication. This sociogram shows how individuals with low thresholds influence those with higher thresholds.

The sociogram in Figure 7.4 displays network relations and diffu-sion thresholds (both relative to system and network) simultaneously so that the flow of adoption influence is readily apparent. For example, woman number 13 is obviously an important source of information for other women in the network given that she adopts early relative to the sys-tem and her network, and she receives numerous network nominations. Woman number 59 adopts relatively early by first using family planning in 1966; however, she is a late adopter in her personal network and so is not a source of influence in the network.

Another model that combined threshold and critical mass effects into a single classification scheme was introduced. This T/CM model yields three adopter categories: zero, low, and high T/CM adopters. The empirical results revealed that low T/CM adopters had more extra-system contact in the medical doctors and Korean women datasets. For the Brazilian farmers, zero T/CM adopters had the highest external system contact scores.

Opinion leadership scores followed the same pattern for the T/CM categories. That is, low T/CM adopters received the most network nomina-tions, except for the Brazilian farmers dataset in which zero T/CM farmers received the most. It was concluded that low T/CM adopters were the opinion leaders for the medical doctors and Korean women, but zero T/CM adopters were the leaders for the Brazilian farmers.

This chapter has provided support for the interpersonal influence model outlined throughout this book. Network thresholds provide the abil-ity to understand the interpersonal influence process during the diffusion of innovations. Given the different results for the Brazilian farmers, one possible interpretation is that the extra-system contact enabled farmers to

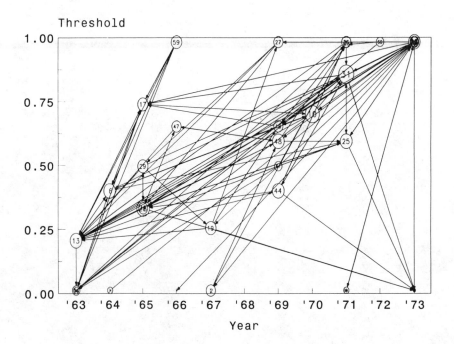

Figure 7.4. Thresholds and network nominations for Korean family planning village 24

Note: The y-axis represents threshold values that range form zero to one, and the x-axis represents time of adoption that ranges for 1963 to 1973.

deviate from the network norms more radically than in the other datasets, but this deviation diminished their ability to act as opinion leaders. That is, higher cosmopoliteness and more media sources enabled some farmers to adopt hybrid corn before any of their same status farmers, and yet because they did adopt so much sooner than their peers, their adoption was less likely to be imitated.

Other Network Models and Methods

The threshold models used in Chapter 7 represent one specific combination of threshold and system influences. The present chapter discusses other possible methods useful for understanding network models and contagion and diffusion. The models presented here expand the concept of exposure and introduce alternative means for analyzing it.

The network thresholds presented so far have used one measure of relational and positional influence. The first section discusses in detail how other network weighting schemes permit the modeling of various network and attribute relations in the diffusion process. Specifically, the section discusses how researchers might use physical distance, social status, centrality, or other network weights in threshold computations.

The next section introduces the corrected threshold measure, which is the threshold corrected for the average amount of network exposure at the time of adoption. The corrected threshold measure subtracts average exposure from thresholds to create a single variable that does not vary with time of adoption, yet presents a measure of network thresholds.

Then, the next section presents event history analysis, introducing this technique and showing how it is used in diffusion of innovations research. Results from the event history analysis are presented and show that network exposure is not related to innovation adoption. The final section provides dyadic analysis that again shows that network exposure is not related to innovativeness. Event history and dyadic analyses demonstrate the importance of network thresholds and thus argue for the primacy of the threshold concepts presented in this book.

115

OTHER THRESHOLD MODELS

The general framework of network exposure with various weights construct-ed from network indices and computation of a threshold value based on time of adoption can be adapted to many theoretical perspectives. The model could be constructed using Hägerstrand's notion that physical dis-tance acts as a measure of influence. Physical distance would then be a measure of the probability that two persons come into contact and influence one another. The sociomatrix is a measure of the physical distance that per-sons are from one another. Also, Karlsson's (1958) notion of social distance as the sociomatrix could be used as the who-to-whom sociomatrices.

Network weights may be used with the network nomination matrix to model various network influences. For example, centrality is an important influence on adoption behavior (see Chapters 3 and 4) and hence can be used as a network weight on exposure. One test of the opin-ion leader model would be to weight exposure by centrality (the measure of opinion leadership) scores. Such a weighting scheme posits that individ-uals are more strongly influenced by those with higher centrality.

Thresholds can then be computed from weighted exposure matri-ces and correlated with explanatory variables. If opinion leadership does work through its influence in social networks, the weighted thresholds should be more highly correlated with explanatory variables. The analysis shows that this is not the case. Correlations or other measures of associa-tion between explanatory variables and centrality weighted thresholds are no stronger than thresholds computed on direct ties.

It may well be that a more complicated weighting scheme involv-ing centrality and other network characteristics could be developed. For example, simply multiplying centrality by direct ties may not be the best means to model network influence. Other threshold models can be con-structed from the exposure and network information. For example, central-ity betweenness can be multiplied by structural equivalence to model the simultaneous influence of opinion leadership and positional equivalence. Individuals are influenced most by those who are in a similar position and more popular. Countless combinations are possible depending on the sub-stantive issue at hand.

Moreover, other explanatory variables may be brought into the analysis. Much social theory argues that individuals imitate the behavior of those just above themselves in the status hierarchy. We could weight net-work ties on education, income, expertise, or some scale of SES attributes to model this influence. Consequently, a vast range of network weighting schemes in combination with each other and with other explanatory vari-ables may be used to model interpersonal influence in the diffusion of innovations.

All of these various weighting schemes provide threshold values that show whether an individual required low or high levels of this influence to adopt an innovation. In addition to network weighting schemes, it is possible to construct a corrected threshold score that corrects for the level of network exposure in the system.

CORRECTED THRESHOLDS

A parsimonious means to disentangle the relationship between thresholds and exposure is to subtract average exposure from thresholds. Subtracting average exposure from thresholds yields a corrected threshold measure. *Corrected thresholds* take into account the level of network exposure in the social system at the time of adoption. Corrected thresholds are thresholds minus average network exposure. The corrected threshold measure indicates the degree to which individuals deviate from system norms. Individuals with high or low corrected thresholds deviate considerably from the average system behavior based on their personal network and predisposition to adopt the innovation.

Specifically, individuals with high corrected thresholds adopt early when average exposure is low, yet their personal network exposure is high. Thus, they are early adopters relative to the whole network, yet late adopters relative to their personal network. In the same way that thresholds represent a measure of personal network innovativeness that can be contrasted with system-level innovativeness, the corrected threshold is one measure that captures the degree of innovativeness vis-à-vis both system and personal network.

Figure 8.1 graphs the corrected thresholds for community 24 of the Korean family planning study. The corrected thresholds represent the degree individual thresholds deviate from average exposure. High corrected thresholds, above the zero line, represent innovativeness relative to system; low corrected thresholds, below the zero line, represent innovativeness relative to one's personal network. Influences on adoption correlated with corrected threshold will indicate whether those influences operate to make individuals innovative relative to their whole community or just their personal network.

In the Korean family planning data, corrected thresholds are negatively correlated with education, indicating that those with high education have low corrected thresholds. The correlation between education and corrected thresholds indicates that education is associated with innovativeness relative to personal networks. This is also true for exposure to a campaign to promote family planning. Individuals exposed to the campaign were more likely to have low corrected thresholds, thus indicating

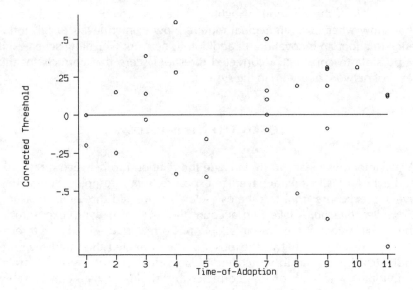

Figure 8.1. Corrected thresholds for Korean family planning village 24 which shows each individual's threshold less the average exposure for the social system at that time period

Note: Individuals with scores above zero line have high personal thresholds; their personal network has more adopters than average when they adopt. Individuals below the zero line are innovative relative to their personal network.

their willingness to adopt before their peers. In the Brazilian farmers dataset, use of numerous sources of information for agricultural information led to lower corrected thresholds.

Thus, the corrected threshold provides a convenient measure of system versus personal network innovativeness. It should be noted that the corrected threshold is not associated with time of adoption, and the present results were computed by controlling for time of adoption by entering it as a variable in the regression equations.

EVENT HISTORY ANALYSIS

Prior research (Marsden & Podolny, 1990) has argued that network exposure was not related to adoption of innovation. By constructing an exposure measure similar to that presented here, Marsden argued that high exposure did not lead to adoption. Marsden used event history analysis to test the effect of exposure on time of adoption. Event history analysis is a statistical technique used to study dynamic processes (Tuma & Hannan, 1984). Event history analysis is appropriate for studying diffusion because it addresses two principle problems which occur in the study of the diffusion of innovations: censoring and time-varying variables (Allison, 1984; Strang, 1990, 1991).

Censoring occurs when data collection of a variable results in the measure of the variable being inaccurately recorded. In diffusion studies, time of adoption is recorded at the time of the study, however, many individuals do not adopt the innovation at the time of the study. Therefore, these individuals are assigned a time of adoption as the time of study, yet we do not know when or even if they adopted.[1] Event history analysis techniques were developed to address this problem in data collection.

The second difficulty encountered in diffusion research is time-varying variables. Time-varying variables vary in their values over time. For example, education influences time of adoption, yet education is a variable whose value changes over time because some individuals acquire more education during the course of an innovation's diffusion.

The present book has introduced an exposure variable that varies during the course of an innovation's diffusion. Thus, exposure is a time-varying variable that generally increases over time. At each time period during the course of an innovation's diffusion, individuals possess an exposure value that will usually increase at the next time period.

Event history analysis corrects problems of censoring and time-varying variables by constructing a new dataset from an existing dataset. The new dataset is a case-by-time period dataset in which each individual contributes a case for each time period they did not adopt, and one for their time of adoption.

For example, if an individual adopts at time period six, their representation in the new dataset would be six cases: One for each time period they did not adopt and the time period of adoption. The dependent variable of adoption is converted to a binary variable such that each case (person-time) receives a zero until the case representing adoption. That case receives a one. If the case is censored—did not adopt by the end of the study—then the last case retains a zero. Both time-varying and time-constant variables may be included in this new dataset.

For example, suppose an individual adopted at time period five with a threshold of 60%. His or her exposure would increase during the first five time periods until adoption, when it would reach 60%. The exposure values increase from 0% to 60%, and each value is represented in the new dataset. Additionally, variables that do not vary over time are included in each new case with its value.

---

[1]This is referred to as right-censoring because the censoring occurs on the right side of a timeline.

To determine the influence of exposure and education on adoption, maximum likelihood logistic regression (Eliason, 1993) is used with the binary adoption variable as dependent and network exposure, as well as other non-time-varying independent variables, as independent variables. Such an analysis was conducted on the present datasets to determine if exposure influenced adoption.

The results show that exposure is not related to adoption. Network exposure, whether through wide or narrow lenses of social contacts and whether through cohesion or structural equivalence, does not influence adoption of innovations. That is, the exposure variables computed from direct ties, as well as ties of ties in the cohesion context, do not influence adoption of innovations. Exposure computed from the structural equivalence matrix raised to low or high powers (2, 4, 8, or 16) also does not influence adoption of innovations. This result is consistent with other event history analysis (Marsden & Podolny, 1990; Strang, 1990) and indicates that interpersonal network exposure does not lead to innovation adoption.

The lack of association between network exposure and adoption requires careful scrutiny. Diffusion theory has always specified that adopters interact with nonadopters, and this interaction leads to adoption. In other words, the interpersonal contact between individuals is essential for effective diffusion of an innovation. The fact that network exposure does not influence adoption may put this basic axiom in doubt.

However, exposure's noninfluence on adoption reaffirms the primacy placed here on thresholds. Thresholds are the point at which an individual's interpersonal exposure is sufficient to lead to adoption behavior. Thresholds are distributed throughout the population so that individuals with low thresholds adopt when their exposure is low. Individuals with low thresholds do not wait until their exposure is higher to adopt, but rather, adopt when their exposure is low. Consequently, exposure cannot influence adoption in the traditional manner in which higher exposure is expected to be correlated with adoption. Rather, exposure influences adoption by enabling individuals to reach their thresholds.

Hazard Rates

Hazard rates are numbers that indicate the probability an event will occur during a specified time period (see Teachman & Hayward, 1993; Tuma & Hannan, 1984). Hazard rates are computed in event history analysis by computing the proportion of individuals who adopted from the population of those available to adopt. Specifically, the hazard rate for each time period is the number of adopters divided by the number still at risk to adopt.

For example, the hazard rates for the first two time periods of the medical innovation data community (Peoria) are .08 and .07 (5 and 4 adopters). These rates are computed as follows: Five individuals adopt at time period one, thus the hazard rate at time period one is .08 (5/62). Because five have adopted by time period one, they are no longer eligible to adopt the innovation, and hence the set of individuals at risk to adopt at time period two is 57 (62-5), and the hazard rate is the number of adopters divided by the number at risk, .07 (4/57).

The average hazard rates across communities for each study are shown in Figure 8.2. Notice how different the hazard rates vary between studies. The medical innovation hazard rates increase for the first six time periods, showing an increasing tendency to adopt the innovation. After time period six, the proportion of adopters drops off. For the Brazilian farmers, the probability to adopt is very low until time period 10, then the adoption probabilities begin to climb upward until the time of data collection. For the Korean family planning study, adoption probabilities are almost constant until one year prior to data collection. At that time, 1972, a greater proportion of Korean women adopted family planning than during any other year. These hazard rates again emphasize the difference in diffusion patterns.

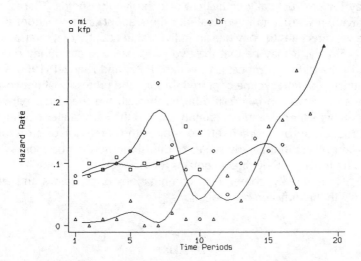

Figure 8.2. Hazard rates for the three studies averaged across communities

Note: The hazard rates indicate the proportion of adopters computed from those still eligible to adopt at each time period. Notice how an individual is likely to adopt the innovation early in the medical innovation study (top graph), and the hazard rate peaks by time period six. In contrast, the Brazilian farmers do not have high probability of adoption until very late, and for Korean women, the probability of adoption is almost steady across all 10 years.

COMPLEMENTARITY

Demonstrating that cohesion and structural equivalence may each be active in the spread of innovations indicates that there is some complementarity in their functioning. Specifically, cohesion and structural equivalence are not exclusive interpersonal influence forces, but rather act simultaneously to influence adoption behavior. Indeed, it is not at all surprising to say that individuals monitor their environment and are influenced by both those with whom they have direct contact and those who occupy similar positions in their role relations. Cohesion and structural equivalence may complement one another in at least three ways.

First, it may be that awareness of innovations flows through cohesive ties as individuals talk to one another, but adoption is more likely to occur through modeling the behavior of near peers (structurally equivalent others). Such a scenario is highly likely given that individuals do receive considerable information through their network of direct contacts. However, they may hesitate to adopt an innovation until they see others similar to themselves adopt it.

Second, adoption by either cohesive or structurally equivalent others may lower structurally equivalent or cohesive thresholds. That is, once an individual's structurally equivalent others adopt an innovation, it may take fewer direct ties to convince an individual to adopt, or vice versa.

Finally, it may be that the two processes operate during different stages in the diffusion process. Coleman, Katz, and Menzel (1966) found that diffusion of tetracycline occurred through the professional networks of advice and discussion before it diffused through the friendship networks. Given that greater risk and uncertainty exist in the early stages of diffusion, individuals may be more likely to model the behavior of structurally equivalent others in the early stages of diffusion and then be more willing later to be influenced by direct contacts (or vice versa).

Undoubtedly, some or all combinations of processes and effects are likely in the diffusion of innovations.

DYADS

The analysis thus far in this book has focused on personal, group, and system-level influences on adoption. However, the adoption decision-making process may also be viewed as one in which individuals monitor the behavior of their dyadic partners. In other words, each individual can be seen as having a set of contacts each of which consists of distinct communication and comparison processes.

For such analysis, the unit of analysis is the dyad. A dyad is a relation between two individuals. In dyadic analysis the set of all possible
relations in a social system is considered the sample such that, if *n* is the
size of the population, the sample size equals *n* (*n* - 1). The network size is
multiplied by the set of all possible relations; then the self nominations are
subtracted. For example, in a community of 35 individuals there are 1,190
dyadic relations: 35(34). For our purposes, the relevant variable to predict
is no longer earliness of innovation measured by time of adoption, but
rather, whether two individuals adopt an innovation at the same time.

That is, because we are concerned with the dyad, we want to know
whether the dyad exhibits similarity in adoption times. Two individuals
might adopt an innovation at the same time due to: (a) their influence on
each other, (b) their influence from the same factors, and (c) chance.
Adoption similarity is the degree two individuals adopt at the same time.
Adoption similarity is constructed by using a time of adoption vector for a
community and taking the absolute value difference for all possible pairs
and subtracting this from the maximum possible adoption time. Two individuals who adopt at the same time have zero difference, and this subtracted
from the maximum time of adoption yields the maximum time of adoption.

Adoption similarity for all possible pairs was constructed for the
three datasets, and these values correlated with the cohesion and structural equivalence values for each pair.[2] The dyadic network analysis does not
let us distinguish between factors (a) and (b) because individuals may
exhibit influence from dyadic partners, yet be influenced by the same factors. However, the dyadic analysis will eliminate chance adoption similarity by correlating similarity of adoption times with cohesion and structural
equivalence scores. For the three datasets, adoption similarity was correlated with cohesion for medical innovation ($r = -.05$, $p < .001$); both cohesion and ($r = .02$, $p < .001$) and SE ($r = .05$, $p < .001$) for Brazilian farmers;
and SE ($r = .03$, $p < .001$) for Korean family planners.

The pattern of association seen here indicates that dyadic influences may be present, and if so, they are extremely weak. Dyadic analysis
yields large sample sizes because the sample size is the set of all possible
pairs. So, the correlations coefficients are significant, but they are very
small. The negative association between adoption similarity and cohesion
in the medical innovation data indicates that individuals who are near
relationally (low geodesics) have similar adoption times (high adoption
similarity scores). This is not true for Brazilian farmers; they had positive
correlations between adoption similarity and both geodesics and SE. Thus,
nearness was associated with adoption *dissimilarity*, and SE (nearness sta-

---

[2]The adoption similarity, geodesic, and structural equivalence matrices were created, then converted into long vectors by staking each column. These vectors then
constituted a dataset of dyadic relations.

tuswise) was associated with adoption similarity. For Korean family planning, SE was associated with adoption similarity.

The greater associations for SE versus cohesion indicates that individuals may be more influenced at the dyadic level by structurally equivalent others. In other words, when it comes to imitating the behavior of others, that other may be structurally equivalent when that "other" refers to only one person. Moreover, at the dyadic level of analysis, two structurally equivalent individuals are likely to have more secondary factors in common that simultaneously influence adoption behavior. Indeed, SE is much more associated with adoption similarity for the various communities of the Brazilian and Korean datasets.

Thus, when we compare individuals and treat them as dyads, their adoption similarity is more likely to be associated with structural equivalence than with direct relations. To be sure, this association is weak, and the conclusion is that it is just as likely to be a product of behavior modeling as it is to be a product of similar external influences. It is possible that individuals are better at modeling SE influences when they consider one other individual but are more influenced by direct ties when considered as aggregate influences. In other words, an individual may be strongly influenced to adopt an innovation by one SE other, but not by a whole group of them, because if it was a whole group, then that individual would most likely be connected to that group and have direct relations with those members.

SUMMARY

The present chapter has discussed other weighting schemes that might be used in modeling network thresholds. Other weights such as centrality or radiality could be used to model the greater influence these individuals have in the network. Additionally, one could use attributional factors in conjunction with network structure to create more complex weighting schemes. For example, SES can be multiplied by an adjacency matrix to model the influence higher SES individuals have on network exposure. A wide variety of network weighting schemes are thus possible.

The next section discussed the creation of a corrected threshold measure that combines simultaneously innovativeness relative to the system and to one's personal network. The corrected threshold measure controls for the system-level network exposure at the time of adoption and thus represents a more parsimonious measure useful when one wishes to disentangle system versus personal network effects.

The subsequent section three presented an event history analysis of exposure's effect on adoption. Event history analysis is useful for modeling censoring and time-varying variables that are important in studying the diffusion of innovations. The event history analysis showed that network exposure is not related to adoption. The lack of association between network exposure and adoption indicates how important thresholds are in the study of diffusion. Network exposure is important because it triggers network thresholds, not because more exposure leads to more adoption.

Finally, dyadic analysis was conducted to determine how individuals model the behavior of others in their network when considered individually. The dyadic analysis consisted of determining whether individuals' adoption similarity was correlated with distance through direct ties and distance through structural equivalence. The results showed that adoption similarity was extremely weakly correlated with both these distance measures, although the effect was slightly stronger for structural equivalence.

Conclusions and Discussions

This chapter provides a summary of the main theoretical and empirical conclusions drawn from the theoretical perspectives and empirical results presented in this book. The various applications of network diffusion models are discussed. The discussion centers around how diffusion networks, threshold, and critical mass theory can be applied to mass media campaigns, markets and economies, interactive communication technology, public opinion, and policy analysis.

The next section contrasts network threshold and critical mass theories with the traditional model of diffusion of innovations. Specifically, the network theory is compared and contrasted with the traditional diffusion model to show how the approaches differ. The network theory of diffusion provides different adopter categories and a better ability to predict the diffusion of innovations by modeling contagion. Finally, the last section provides conclusions from the theoretical perspectives and empirical analysis of Chapters 3 through 8.

APPLICATIONS

This section covers areas of application for network, threshold, and critical mass models of diffusion. The potential applications for the models are divided into: (a) mass media campaigns, (b) markets and economies, specifically forecasting, (c) interactive communication technology, (d) public opinion, and (e) policy analysis.

127

Mass Media Campaigns

Mass media campaigns are produced to promote the sale of products, encourage prosocial behavior, and generate favorable attitudes toward candidates and ballot issues. The present theory regarding network models, thresholds, and the critical mass can be used to great advantage in understanding the effect of these campaigns. Campaign effects emerge in the interaction between mass media and interpersonal communication (Valente, Kim, Lettenmaier, Glass, & Dibba, 1994).

For example, campaigns designed to promote family planning often result in increasing interpersonal communication about family planning. Measuring the communication network before and after the campaign should show an increase in such measures as social network density, increased network activity among individuals who are satisfied adopters, and less group membership based on adoption status. So, although a post-campaign measure may not show an increase or change in actual use of family planning methods, it may show an increase in interpersonal communication about family planning.

For thresholds, post-campaign measures may indicate that individuals have lowered their threshold for adoption of family planning. A goal of many prosocial campaigns is to make prosocial behaviors normative, that is, to convince individuals that the promoted behavior is a proper one and supported within the culture. As such, individuals should show a decrease in the proportion of network partners needed for an individual to adopt the behavior.

Furthermore, the interplay between social system network and personal network dependencies may be specified. As the present research shows, individuals vary in their susceptibility to social system and peer network influences. Using social system and personal network threshold models, evaluators can determine whether individuals change their personal proportion of adopters for each, and whether they change their perceived susceptibility to these proportions.

For example, a family planning campaign designed to disseminate accurate information about the benefits of family planning may reduce the system-level exposure necessary to adopt family planning. Individuals exposed to the campaign may feel less dependent on system norms for family planning use and thus lower their social system network threshold. This technique is appropriate when adoption levels are low, thus individuals are not likely to be exposed by sufficient adopters in their personal network to reach their personal network threshold. Conversely, in situations in which family planning adoption is reasonably high, say 50-60%, some individuals will have relatively high personal networks of adopters. Such campaigns should encourage interpersonal communication about family planning so individuals are exposed to the family planning behavior of their network partners and realize their threshold (i.e., adopt).

The Population Communication Services project at the School of Public Health, The Johns Hopkins University (JHU/PCS), has made considerable progress in the use of communication to promote family planning. Currently, research is being conducted in Asia, Africa, The Near East, and Latin America to better understand the role of communication networks in promoting family planning. JHU/PCS has shown that using communication networks to promote family planning has accelerated family planning diffusion and created a more hospitable environment for social change (Kincaid, Das Gupta, Mitra, Whitney, Senior, Yun, & Massiah, 1993).

Audience segmentation on network characteristics represents another approach implied by the present research. To promote more rapid dissemination and diffusion, campaigns should be targeted to those individuals who insure the swiftest diffusion after their adoption. Opinion leaders, often operationalized as those most central, would be best targeted to serve this role in campaigns. However, centrals are often dependent on system norms and may be reluctant to adopt a new idea, opinion, or product if it contradicts existing norms. However, the present research shows that another effective means to achieve critical mass is to have early adoption by radials.

Radial individuals have more extensive, broad reaching ties than nonradials (those in more personally dense/integrated networks). Radials provide weak ties that bridge clusters or groups in the network. As such, radials often represent the only link between various factions in a network. If radials adopt early or support an innovation early in its diffusion, diffusion occurs more rapidly and more extensively (to a larger proportion of the network). Currently, the best measure in existence for measuring radiality and centrality simultaneously is centrality betweenness.

Centrality betweenness measures the volume of network contacts as well as the degree an individual lies on the shortest path connecting all pairs of possible people in the network. Consequently, early adoption by betweenness centrals represents the best mechanism to accelerate diffusion. Radials are likely to be early adopters presumably because they are less tied to any one group's norms and are also more likely to receive novel information and influence earlier.

The important part about media campaigns is that individuals act based on their perceptions of what the group or system will do. Often those perceptions are filtered by influential members of one's network—those individuals who are perceived to be "in touch" with "what's happening." Radials often serve this function because network members rightly perceive radials to be more in touch with a broader array of others in the network.

Radials have greater external system contact in their network due to the range of network contacts. Thus radials serve as an important bridge between external contact and the network. Our results have shown that those with low thresholds tend to have greater external system contact, which is generated by either cosmopolitan behavior or by use of formal media channels to gain information. Thus, the two-step flow of media influence finds rigorous definition in network models of diffusion.

Markets and Economies

Another application of network threshold models is through improved forecasting of the spread of innovations. As an innovation spreads, threshold levels for early adopters may be computed. If these early thresholds are uniformly low, that is, individuals are adopting before many of their personal network adopt, then diffusion can be expected to occur rapidly. If early adopters register high thresholds, this indicates high resistance to adoption, and thus diffusion will occur more slowly.

The high resistance retards diffusion and slows it down. The advantage to measuring thresholds is that it provides the opportunity to study the diffusion process while it occurs. Discovering resistance permits planners and innovators the opportunity to adjust the product or campaign to address this resistance. Moreover, the resistance can be used to predict accurate levels of demand.

For example, the introduction of a new product may have early adopters with low or high threshold. If the early adopters have low personal network thresholds, subsequent diffusion levels can be estimated by extrapolating a diffusion function. However, if personal network thresholds of early adopters are high, research can determine the cause for this high resistance or alternatively adjust production schedules for the revised levels of demand.

Additionally, including network characteristics in diffusion forecasting will result in more accurate predictions. The same innovation will diffuse more rapidly in a dense network than a sparse one. Forecasts for the growth of the number of consumers is done by selecting a rate parameter and estimating how fast the function will grow. This rate parameter can be adjusted to include network characteristics.

Because the presence of radial individuals accelerates diffusion, the rate of diffusion for an innovation can be linked to the average radiality of the networks. An innovation might be introduced into numerous organizations at the same time. Organizations with more radials can be expected to experience a faster rate of adoption. Thus, more accurate adoption levels at later points in time may be estimated.

Interactive Communication Technologies

Interactive communication technologies represent media of high interdependence, and as such, are subject to higher network, threshold, and critical mass effects. The present model provides an excellent framework to view interactive communication technology. Specifically, the threshold model is appropriate for studying why and how individuals and organizations decide when to adopt an electronic communication tool. Moreover, network exposure may determine which standard an individual or organization may decide to use.

Interactive communication technologies provide an excellent opportunity for data collection. Because most electronic network systems retain logs of who communicates with whom, longitudinal communication network data are reliably collected for the researcher (Rice, 1982, 1990). Researchers who are also able to collect time-of-adoption data may replicate and extend the analysis conducted here.

Public Opinion

One area of public opinion research ripe for threshold study is pluralistic ignorance. *Pluralistic ignorance* is the incorrect perception of what constitutes majority and minority opinion on an issue. Often individuals report that the proportion of people in a social system who favor a stance on an issue is high when in fact the proportion is low. But some individuals may actually be reporting majority opinion accurately based on their personal network opinion level. That is, some individuals may report that majority opinion is X when in fact it is Y. However, for some of those classified as pluralistically ignorant, they are in fact pluralistically accurate because for them their personal network of contacts do represent X proportion who hold such an opinion.

By analyzing the overall network structure of opinions we can determine the degree of exposure to a particular opinion for all individuals. This exposure can be calculated for various gradations of the network (direct ties, second step ties, third, etc.) For example, we ask 100 people whether they support amendment X, and 60 say yes and 40 say no. Then we ask what proportion they think supports X.

Individuals who respond that community support is 80% or 90% are pluralistically ignorant. However, from the network exposure perspective, some of these individuals will be pluralistically accurate if their network exposure is 80% or 90%. Indeed, the network perspective yields an array of pluralistic ignorance measures based on the degree individuals deviate in opinions and perceptions from their network context.

What characterizes individuals who hold an opinion is spite of network exposure to the contrary? To what degree is opinion formation contagious? If it is contagious, does it spread through cohesion or structural equivalence?

One of the main conclusions of Chapter 7 was that thresholds provide insight into the two-step flow hypothesis. That is, individuals with low thresholds adopt opinions relatively early and then influence those with higher thresholds. Additional studies could shed considerable light on this process.

Policy Analysis

At the policy level, threshold and critical mass models indicate that more rapid diffusion occurs when proponents of the innovation are central in the network. Consequently, social change policies should be directed at these individuals. Considerable government and private resources are spent to change behavior among a target population. Reaching a critical mass is important, and this research shows how to locate that critical mass.

Virtually all program evaluations ignore the crucial role of network influences on behavioral adoption. Analysis of how the social structure of communication behavior influences policy outcomes and the success or failure of planned policy changes represents an increasingly advantageous manner in which to conduct appropriate evaluation that considers the cultural context of programs.

In summary, these areas of application represent a broad spectrum of uses for the network, threshold, and critical mass models presented here. The network models differ from the traditional diffusion model that has been a mainstay of social change theory for over 30 years. The network exposure model differs from the classic diffusion model in a number of ways that are reviewed in the following section.

CONTRASTING NETWORK THRESHOLDS
WITH THE CLASSIC DIFFUSION MODEL

The network approach is contrasted with the classic diffusion model to bring the network model into sharp relief. Table 9.1 shows the major differences between the classic diffusion model and the network exposure model. First, the classic model creates five adopter categories based on an individual's time of adoption. In contrast, the network exposure diffusion model creates four categories of thresholds based on an individual's innovativeness relative to his or her personal network.

In fact, as we saw in Chapters 7 and 8, the network threshold model can be used to create numerous adopter categories, not just those based on time of adoption. For example, network thresholds can be computed on cohesive and structurally equivalent ties. Network thresholds can also be created for near and distant ties, in a combined threshold/critical mass model, and corrected for the level of exposure in the social system. These network threshold measures capture innovativeness relative to the social system and personal network. Thus, the network exposure model provides a broader array of innovativeness measures.

Second, the classic model developed five stages during the course of innovation diffusion: awareness, persuasion, trial, adoption, and consolidation. The network exposure model provides two stages: pre- and postcritical mass. The network exposure model focuses on the micro process of diffusion and so will probably not develop a more compelling adoption stage scheme than that used in the past.

Third, the classic model provides a description of the diffusion process without providing a means to predict who will be the next individual to adopt an innovation. The network exposure model, however, provides the means to predict both micro- and macrolevel diffusion process-

Table 9.1. The Classic and Network Exposure Diffusion Models.

Concept	Classic Diffusion	Network Exposure
Adopter Categories	innovators	
	early adopters	very low thresholds
	early majority	low thresholds
	late majority	high thresholds
	laggards	very high thresholds
Stages	awareness	precritical mass
	persuasion	postcritical mass
	trial	
	adoption	
	consolidation	
Process	descriptive	predictive
Contagion	positions and relations treated equivalently constant radius of influence equal to the system	positions and relations treated distinctly radius of influence varied from immediate to distant peers

es. The network exposure model permits the specification of what degree of exposure every individual will have during the course of the diffusion and predicts which individuals will likely adopt due to that exposure.

Finally, the classic model treated positional and cohesive ties similarly, that is, it did not differentiate the various roles of contagion discussed in the network exposure model. The network exposure model specifically modeled the role of contagion in the diffusion of innovations. This book has been dedicated to understanding the "diffusion effect," which typically only receives passing acknowledgement in other texts on the diffusion of innovations.

CONCLUSION

One of the principal questions we sought to answer was: Are individuals more influenced by their immediate network partners (whether through cohesion or structural equivalence) or are they more influenced by the adoption behavior of the social system?

It is virtually impossible to answer this question clearly. The myriad of influence an individual receives regarding adoption behavior are extensive. Much interpersonal communication about innovation may be negative; individuals may be smart by waiting to adopt after their peers adopt to gain from their experience, or they may reject the innovation. We do know, however, how early or late an individual's adoption is relative to both the social system and his or her network partners. We can take these measures as manifestations and indicators for *adoption leadership.*

We may never be able to disentangle adoption behavior by "getting inside the head" of adopters. What events, behaviors, or conditions trigger the decision to adopt something? We do know that, in the aggregate, many of these influences are the same for all individuals, and yet some respond by adopting earlier and others by adopting later. Additionally, some individuals adopt early relative to everyone and relative to their immediate peers.

The history of research on the diffusion of innovations has been a gradual recognition of the role of personal networks in influencing adoption behavior. Threshold models posit that individuals have thresholds of adoption at which interpersonal influence is effective at persuading them to adopt. Critical mass models posit that social systems have a critical point of adoption at which the system is self-sustaining.

The major conclusions to be drawn are that network characteristics are associated with adoption behavior at both the individual and system level of analysis. In Chapter 3, opinion leadership, as measured by the number of nominations received, was shown to be correlated with early adoption of innovations. Personal network radiality was also correlated with early adoption. Social system network density was associated with more rapid diffusion. Personal network exposure is highly correlated with adoption because this measure is constructed from time-of-adoption information.

In Chapter 4 it was shown that centrality is weakly correlated with early adoption. The Korean family planning study showed the strongest correlation with time of adoption, which was still only .2. Network centralization was also shown to be highly correlated with rate and prevalence of adoption. More centralized networks had faster diffusion for advantageous innovations and slower diffusion for less obviously advantageous innovations. We then constructed a structural equivalence network exposure model also shown to be highly correlated with time of adoption.

Chapter 5 presented the network threshold model in which it was demonstrated that a normal distribution of thresholds required some other factor to propel diffusion to reach all members of the social system. Thus, some force—mass media, interpersonal communication, or personal predispositions—generally operates on thresholds. The network threshold model was generalized to include various levels of contagion and to account for both cohesion and positional influences.

Chapter 6 presented a discussion of the critical mass. The critical mass was presented as inflection points and as network or attributional properties of the network. Possible means to test the critical mass were presented in addition to arguing that the critical mass is composed of early adoption by betweenness centrality individuals. Empirical evidence showing the correlation between early adoption by betweenness centrals and the rate and spread of diffusion were presented.

Chapter 7 presented empirical analyses of threshold models. The analyses showed how network and system-level thresholds covaried and the role external influence played in the diffusion of innovations. Moreover, the threshold analysis showed how the innovation flowed through the system and how low threshold individuals influenced higher threshold adopters. The chapter also presented one means to combine thresholds and the critical mass into one general model that provided specification of the two-step flow hypothesis.

Finally, Chapter 8 presented alternative network exposure analysis by presenting a discussion of network weighting schemes. Also, event history analysis and dyadic analysis were conducted to show that network exposure does not lead to early adoption, but rather network exposure provides the mechanism for thresholds to be activated.

The accumulated results presented here for network models of innovation diffusion are impressive. However, there are shortcomings to this modeling as well as this research. These shortcomings are unavoidable in some cases, and in other cases represent oversimplifications of complex processes.

LIMITATIONS

The most severe limitation of the present study concerns the relative accuracy of the data. Few datasets have both time-of-adoption and social network data. In an ideal setting, both variables would be measured with precision, over time, and with very few missing data.[1] Although the present data are adequate for testing the feasibility of the threshold model, like most theories future research would benefit from more data.

To collect time-of-adoption and network data generally requires networks of less than 200 potential adopters whose social network and adoption behavior can be measured accurately. Ideally, a few such communities would be studied simultaneously as in the studies analyzed here.

Second, the data may contain errors in the time-of-adoption variable. The time of adoption of the medical drug was collected by the Columbia University Bureau of Applied Social Research investigators by randomly choosing three days per month on which to check the prescription records. Some prescriptions may have been filled on a day that was not sampled, thus missing a drug prescription. Given this data collection strategy, some doctors may have received later adoption times than actual (no doctor could receive an earlier adoption time than actual).

The Brazil and Korea datasets relied on recall of time of adoption. There may be considerable error in this variable because individuals may not remember accurately when they adopted family planning or planted hybrid seed corn. Additionally, individuals may bias their recollection of when they adopted to appear more innovative. Conversely, some studies have shown that these data are indeed accurate (Coughenour, 1965; Nischan, Ebeling, Thomas, & Hirsch, 1993).

FUTURE RESEARCH

The agenda for future research for network threshold models of diffusion of innovations should include: (a) cognitive perceptions of thresholds and critical mass; (b) discovery of counter examples such as rumors that diffuse but do not have threshold effects; (c) differences in exposure level distributions for different innovations (mono- versus polymorphism in thresholds); (d) cognitive components that cause changes in individual thresholds; (e) how to model use and discontinuance; (f) assumptions made about the

---

[1]For example, in each of the four communities of the medical innovation data there were numerous participants (doctors) mentioned as discussion, advice, or friendship network partners. However, adoption data were not collected or were not available for these partners. The influence of these missing respondents is unknown. The Brazil and Korea datasets were less biased in this regard.

critical mass and the implications of these assumptions; and (g) additional analysis of alternate network models.

First, to what degree do cognitive perceptions of thresholds and critical mass exist? The literature reviewed in Chapter 2 addressed how individuals behave based on perceptions of society, public opinion, social status, and so on. Pluralistic ignorance and the spiral of silence theory both argue that perceptions about majority and minority opinions, whether objectively right or wrong, influence behavior. Two major questions emerge: Do individuals perceive threshold and critical mass effects? If so, how accurate are those perceptions?

Second, theory building requires the existence of *counterexamples*, examples that highlight incidences in which the theory is not applicable. Rumors reach a critical mass, yet there is little theoretical reason to believe that any threshold effect occurs. What are examples of other diffusion situations in which the network threshold framework does not apply?

Third, we need to research a variety of innovations to determine *differences in exposure level distributions for different innovations*. How do exposure levels, thresholds and the critical mass differ for different innovations? In other words, how do threshold and critical mass effects change according to the innovation studied?

Additional studies can be conducted to determine whether thresholds are mono- or polymorphic. A *monomorphic threshold* is the degree of network exposure needed to persuade an individual to adopt one innovation. In contrast, a *polymorphic threshold* is the degree of network exposure needed to persuade an individual to adopt many innovations. Specifically, we are concerned with whether an individual who has a low threshold with regard to one innovation is more likely to have a low threshold for other innovations. To be sure, some innovations are bundled such that adoption of one leads to adoption of others. A person has to buy a computer before he or she can buy software and peripherals.[2]

The question is: Do individuals have low or high thresholds for a variety of innovations. Polymorphic threshold variables could be created that more accurately measure the threshold concept. Moreover, researchers can determine whether individuals consistently monitor network behavior at the same levels of influence (i.e., immediate ties, second step ties, third step ties, etc.).

Fourth, we need to address the *cognitive components that cause changes in individual thresholds*. Thresholds shift according to prevailing economic or social conditions. Some traditional societies find adoption of

---

[2]Such conditional purchases leads to discussion of conditional thresholds, which are threshold levels computed on the existence of some attribute. For example, I might have a high threshold to purchases of kitchen supplies unless they happen to be made with cow prints.

new ideas threatening, yet suddenly some innovations diffuse rather widely within these societies. What accounts for these shifts in social norms?

Fifth, not all diffusion processes are all-or-none situations. There are numerous innovation diffusion processes that are based on degree of use. Research needs to determine a means to model use diffusion and determine the ability to test threshold and critical mass effects in use of an innovation (Barnett, Fink, & Debus, 1989). The present research addressed binary adoption decisions, in which individuals either adopted or did not adopt. However, a great many innovation diffusion situations occur that require individuals to continually reassess their decision to adopt. Most consumer products fall into this category; individuals must continually decide to repurchase products or switch to another brand.

Furthermore, use diffusion is modeled with exponential functions that do not have inflection points. The lack of an inflection point in an exponential function makes it difficult to estimate the critical mass. Do thresholds occur if the critical mass does not? Do threshold models also make predictions concerning use diffusion? Threshold effects may be stronger for use diffusion situations because threshold levels provide continuing reinforcement for adoption decisions.

Also, because we have an exposure matrix computed over time, we can model discontinuance that simply changes the exposure level when one's network partners discontinue. Indeed, the network exposure model provides a real means to analyze long-term shifts in adoption behavior.

Scholars can address assumptions made about the critical mass and their implications. The present research made assumptions concerning the critical mass that deserve study. Specifically, the critical mass has been equated with the inflection point. Is this correct? As mentioned previously, any seed value that results in saturation can be considered a critical mass. Is there another way to define critical mass?

The use of the inflection point for the critical mass gave us a working measure. Other definitions such as the seed value, or the first group to engage in a behavior, yield operational definitions that are uninteresting. The present research has shown the utility of an operational definition that equates the inflection point with the critical mass. However, other operational definitions should be considered.

For example, we conceive of a critical mass as 50% of adopters, unless the early adopters are prominent, in which case the critical mass could be the first 10%. The operational definition would consist of weightings for each member of the social system based on their network position. Once the system reached participation of a certain weighted proportion, the system would "go critical."

Finally and most importantly, future research might determine the effect of alternate network weighting schemes on threshold models. This book created threshold measures for cohesive and structurally equivalent ties only. Network threshold weights may be computed to more accurately test opinion leader frameworks and compare and contrast network theories.

The integration of 60 years of diffusion research and over 30 years of network analysis provided us with a network threshold model of social change. The network threshold model is dynamic in the sense that it changes over time, and it is dynamic in that it relates individual behavior to system level outcomes. The model fits well with the available empirical evidence and can be extended in many directions.

The threshold model also suggests a broad range of methodological and theoretical avenues to be pursued in future research. Diffusion research has profited from multi- and interdisciplinary attention throughout its history. The strength of the network threshold model is that diffusion research will continue to do so.

Glossary

Cohesion: An individual's set of direct contacts.

Critical Mass: The minimum percentage of participants necessary to sustain an activity.

Exposure: The percentage of adopters in an individual's personal network.

Exposure Distribution: A sample or population of exposure levels for a diffusion process (exposure levels over time).

Geodesic: The shortest path between two people.

Prevalence: The proportion of adopters in a system.

Saturation: All potential adopters have adopted.

Structural Equivalence: The degree individuals have similar patterns of communication with others in the community (status similarity).

Threshold: The proportion of adopters in an individual's personal network necessary for an individual's to adopt. In other words, a threshold is the exposure level at the time of adoption.

═ Appendix A ═
Gauss Program Which Computes Threshold and Critical Mass Variables

/* DIFFNET.PRG   VERSION 1.2

DIFFNET.PRG, Version 1.2 is a GAUSS386, Version 3.0 program for the analysis of the diffusion of innovations in a social network via the Valente threshold model. The code here contains only core model programming. The complete GAUSS code for the analysis presented in this volume is available from the authors:

Tom Valente and Robert Foreman
JHU/PCS, School of Public Health
527 St. Paul Place
Baltimore, MD 21202
Voice: (410) 659-6367
Fax: (410) 659-6266
Bitnet: TWV_PCS@JHUNIX.HCF.JHU.EDU

The program takes as input a dataset that is a matrix of ID numbers, time of adoption data, and network nominations. The network nominations are converted into a nominations matrix, W (not shown), and the time-of-adoption data are converted into an adoption matrix (ADOPTMAT, shown below).

```
/* COMPUTE ADOPTION MATRIX FROM TOA VECTOR */
"Computing Adoption Matrix...";;
T = maxc(TOA);
ADOPTMAT = zeros(OBS,T);
i = 1;
do while i <= OBS;
        ADOPTMAT[i,TOA[i]:T] = ones(1,T-TOA[i]+1);
        i = i + 1;
endo;
"Done.";

    OUTSTUFF = NG ~ NRPT ~ NMS ~ NS ~ NR ~ NDP;

/* COMPUTE GEODESIC DESIGN(TOA) MATRIX */
"Computing Geodesic Matrix...";;
GEODESIC = diagrv(geod(ADJMAT,OBS-1),zeros(OBS,1));
MAXGEOD = maxc(maxc(GEODESIC));
DESGNTOA = design(TOA);

/* COMPUTE EXPOSURE, THRESHOLD, CORRECTED THRESHOLD,
   AND LAG */

        EXPOSMAT = zeros(OBS,T);
        j = 1;
        do while j <= T;
        EXPOSMAT[.,j] = ((W * ADOPTMAT[.,j]) ./ (sumc(W')+0.01));
        j = j + 1;
        endo;

        /* EXTRACT THRESHOLD FROM EXPOSURE MATRIX */

        THRESH = maxc((DESGNTOA .* EXPOSMAT)');

        /* COMPUTE CORRECTED THRESHOLD */

        EXPOSBAR = meanc(EXPOSMAT);
        CORTHRES = zeros(OBS,1);
        j = 1;
        do while j <= OBS;
        CORTHRES[j] = THRESH[j] - EXPOSBAR[TOA[j]];
```

```
        j = j + 1;
        endo;

        /* COMPUTE LAG: TIME(EXPOSURE REACHES THRESHOLD) -
        TOA */

        THR_TIME = maxindc(((EXPOSMAT - THRESH) .>= 0)');
        LAG = TOA - THR_TIME;

        /* COMPUTE AVERAGE AND ST DEV OF EXPOSURE */

        NAVE = DESGNTOA * meanc(EXPOSMAT);
        NSTD = DESGNTOA * stdc(EXPOSMAT);

/* STICK RESULTS IN OUTSTUFF */

OUTSTUFF = OUTSTUFF ~ THRESH ~ CORTHRES ~ LAG ~ NAVE ~
    NSTD;

                i = i + 1;
                "Done.";
        endo;
endif;

/* EXPOSURE, THRESH, CORRECTED THRESH, AND LAG BY LEVELS */

format /rdn 1,0;
i = 1;
do while i <= 4;

        /* COMPUTE CURRENT LEVEL ADJACENCY MATRIX AND
        "INVERT" IT */
        D = (GEODESIC .* (GEODESIC .<= i));
        disable;
        oldtrol = ndpcntrl(0,0);
        call ndpcntrl(0x0004,0x0004);
        D = 1 ./ D;
        D = missex(D,isnan(D));
        D = missrv(D,0);
        call ndpcntrl(oldtrol,0xffff);
        enable;
        /* COMPUTE EXPOSURE MATRIX */
        EXPOSMAT = zeros(OBS,T);
```

```
           j = 1;
           do while j <= T;
              EXPOSMAT[.,j] = ((D * ADOPTMAT[.,j]) ./ (sumc(D') + 0.01));
                j = j + 1;
           endo;

           /* EXTRACT THRESHOLD FROM EXPOSURE MATRIX */
           THRESH = maxc((DESGNTOA .* EXPOSMAT)');

           /* COMPUTE CORRECTED THRESHOLD */
           EXPOSBAR = meanc(EXPOSMAT);
           CORTHRES = zeros(OBS,1);
           j = 1;
           do while j <= OBS;
                CORTHRES[j] = THRESH[j] - EXPOSBAR[TOA[j]];
                j = j + 1;
           endo;

           /* COMPUTE LAG: TIME(EXPOSURE REACHES THRESHOLD) -
           TOA */
           THR_TIME = maxindc(((EXPOSMAT - THRESH) .>= 0)');
           LAG = TOA - THR_TIME;

           /* COMPUTE AVERAGE AND ST DEV OF EXPOSURE */
           NAVE = DESGNTOA * meanc(EXPOSMAT);
           NSTD = DESGNTOA * stdc(EXPOSMAT);

           /* STICK RESULTS IN OUTSTUFF */
           OUTSTUFF = OUTSTUFF ~ THRESH ~ CORTHRES ~ LAG ~
           NAVE ~ NSTD;
             i = i + 1;
      endo;
      "Done.";

      /* EXPOSURE, THRESH, CORRECTED THRESH, AND LAG BY      v */

      "Computing Burt Threshold Stuff...";;
      /* COMPUTE BURT'S STRUC. EQUIV. WEIGHT MATRIX */

      "D...";;
      Z = GEODESIC / MAXGEOD;
      D = zeros(OBS,OBS);
```

```
i = 1;
do while i <= OBS;
        j = 1;
        do while j <= OBS;
                sum1 = 0;
                sum2 = 0;
                k = 1;
                do while k <= OBS;
                        if ((k /= i) and (k /= j));
                                sum1 = sum1 + (Z[i,k]-Z[j,k])^2;
                                sum2 = sum2 + (Z[k,i]-Z[k,j])^2;
                        endif;
                        k = k + 1;
                endo;
                D[i,j] = sqrt((Z[i,j]-Z[j,i])^2+sum1+sum2);
                j = j + 1;
        endo;
        i = i + 1;
endo;

/* COMPUTE W BY LEVELS OF V */

i = 0;
do while i <= 4;
        v = 2^i;
        print v "... ";;
        W = zeros(OBS,OBS);
        j = 1;
        do while j <= OBS;
        DMAXJ = maxc(D[j,.]');
        k = 1;
        do while k <= OBS;
                sum1 = 0;
                l = 1;
                do while l <= OBS;
                    if (l /= j);
                        sum1 = sum1 + (DMAXJ - D[l,j])^v;
                    endif;
                    l = l + 1;
                endo;
                if (sum1 /= 0);
                    W[j,k] = (DMAXJ - D[k,j])^v / sum1;
                endif;
```

```
                    k = k + 1;
            endo;
            j = j + 1;
    endo;

    W = diagrv(W,zeros(OBS,1));

    /* COMPUTE EXPOSURE MATRIX */
    EXPOSMAT = zeros(OBS,T);
    j = 1;
    do while j <= T;
    EXPOSMAT[.,j] = ((W * ADOPTMAT[.,j]) ./ (sumc(W') + 0.01));
    j = j + 1;
    endo;

    /* EXTRACT THRESHOLD FROM EXPOSURE MATRIX */
    THRESH = maxc((DESGNTOA .* EXPOSMAT)');

    /* COMPUTE CORRECTED THRESHOLD */
    EXPOSBAR = meanc(EXPOSMAT);
    CORTHRES = zeros(OBS,1);
    j = 1;
    do while j <= OBS;
            CORTHRES[j] = THRESH[j] - EXPOSBAR[TOA[j]];
            j = j + 1;
    endo;

    /* COMPUTE LAG: TIME(EXPOSURE REACHES THRESHOLD) -
    TOA */
    THR_TIME = maxindc(((EXPOSMAT - THRESH) .>= 0)');
    LAG = TOA - THR_TIME;

    /* COMPUTE AVERAGE AND ST DEV OF EXPOSURE */
    NAVE = DESGNTOA * meanc(EXPOSMAT);
    NSTD = DESGNTOA * stdc(EXPOSMAT);

    /* STICK RESULTS IN OUTSTUFF */
    OUTSTUFF = OUTSTUFF ~ THRESH ~ CORTHRES ~ LAG ~
    NAVE ~ NSTD;

            i = i + 1;
    endo;
    "Done.";
```

═ **Appendix B** ═

MEDIA SOURCE SCALE FOR BRAZILIAN FARMERS STUDY

Do you regularly receive news about agriculture through:

1. Radio
2. Television
3. Newspaper
4. Magazine
5. Agriculture Bulletin
6. Agronomist or Veterinarian

MASS MEDIA EXPOSURE SCALE FOR KOREAN WOMEN

How often have you heard or seen the family planning program on the following:

	Never	Once	3/year	12/year	Everyday
1. Radio	0	1	2	3	4
2. Television	0	1	2	3	4
3. Newspaper	0	1	2	3	4
4. Magazine	0	1	2	3	4
5. Family Planning Magazine	0	1	2	3	4

CAMPAIGN MEDIA EXPOSURE SCALE FOR KOREAN WOMEN

How often have you heard or seen the family planning program on the following:

	Never	Once	3/year	12/year	Everyday
1. Movie	0	1	2	3	4
2. Poster	0	1	2	3	4
3. Pamphlet	0	1	2	3	4
4. Meeting	0	1	2	3	4
5. Public Lecture	0	1	2	3	4
6. Mobile Van	0	1	2	3	4
7. Neighbors	0	1	2	3	4
8. Field Officer Visit	0	1	2	3	4

= **Appendix C** =

SELECTED SCORES FOR 40 NETWORKS

Comm.	N	Cum Pct	Rate	Net Degr Cent	Net Clos Cent	Net Bet Cent	Net Dens	Ave Ind Degr	Grp.	Pos.
MI 1	62	89	.0047	.24	.28	.14	.04	2.58	ns	ns
2	24	88	.0116	.54	.58	.44	.09	2.17	ns	ns
3	18	81	.0104	.29	.39	.25	.10	2.00	ns	ns
4	21	89	.0151	.39	.39	.18	.13	2.22	ns	ns
BF 10	35	63	.0079	.65	.62	.34	.10	3.34	.01	ns
22	69	29	.0038	.74	.74	.74	.03	1.97	ns	ns
23	60	98	.0062	.19	.32	.30	.04	2.63	.001	ns
24	69	87	.0044	.35	.34	.23	.04	2.83	ns	ns
30	82	91	.0048	.39	.41	.30	.04	2.98	ns	ns
31	75	69	.0034	.4	.42	.31	.04	2.76	ns	ns
43	56	79	.0080	.37	.36	.19	.06	3.09	.01	.01
70	68	93	.0049	.26	.30	.27	.03	2.24	ns	ns
71	70	77	.0047	.41	.39	.31	.04	2.84	ns	ns
80	45	82	.0083	.31	.41	.39	.04	1.84	ns	.05
82	63	86	.0064	.62	.65	.53	.05	3.02	ns	ns
KFP 1	46	74	.0081	.44	.45	.21	.09	4.00	.05	ns
2	59	64	.0045	.29	.33	.21	.07	3.85	.01	ns
3	36	78	.0102	.40	.40	.13	.15	5.42	.05	ns
4	30	70	.009	.33	.32	.08	.19	5.43	ns	ns
5	49	78	.0077	.21	.23	.15	.07	3.20	ns	ns

151

6	44	70	.0073	.39	.38	.23	.08	3.64	ns	ns
7	48	65	.0064	.53	.56	.32	.11	5.02	ns	ns
8	48	54	.005	.56	.51	.32	.08	3.88	.05	ns
9	39	64	.0066	.29	.28	.17	.12	4.46	ns	ns
10	36	83	.0117	.44	.43	.14	.16	5.61	.01	ns
11	38	79	.0107	.31	.32	.09	.14	5.16	ns	ns
12	44	45	.0055	.21	.27	.16	.06	2.61	ns	ns
13	45	69	.0068	.30	.29	.13	.08	3.42	.05	.05
14	39	49	.0052	.45	.42	.16	.14	5.15	ns	ns
15	46	72	.0068	.23	.27	.15	.07	3.11	ns	ns
16	33	70	.0085	.53	.53	.25	.14	4.52	ns	ns
17	45	80	.0084	.37	.44	.30	.08	3.58	ns	ns
18	39	59	.0072	.21	.35	.25	.07	2.51	ns	ns
19	45	56	.0061	.42	.42	.35	.08	3.44	ns	ns
20	28	75	.0107	.24	.25	.12	.10	2.68	ns	ns
21	54	44	.0041	.42	.39	.24	.11	5.70	ns	ns
22	43	49	.0025	.50	.51	.32	.08	3.51	.01	ns
23	34	59	.0065	.51	.50	.34	.11	3.50	ns	ns
24	39	69	.0079	.40	.40	.25	.08	3.03	ns	ns
25	40	52	.0057	.67	.70	.43	.11	4.42	.01	.05

References

Allen, D. (1988). New telecommunications services: Network externalities and critical mass. *Telecommunications Policy, 15,* 257-271.

Allen, D. (1990, March). *Competition, cooperation and critical mass in the evolution of networks.* Paper presented at the International Telecommunications Society, Venice, Italy.

Allison, P.D. (1984). *Event history analysis.* Newbury Park, CA: Sage.

Anderson, J.G., & Jay, S.J. (1985). The diffusion of medical technology: Social network analysis and policy research. *The Sociological Quarterly, 26*(1), 49-64.

Aptech Systems. (1992). GAUSS. Maple Valley, WA: Author.

Arthur, W.B. (1989). Competing technologies, increasing returns, and lock-in by historical events. *The Economic Journal, 99*(394), 116-131.

Arthur, W.B. (1990). Positive feedbacks in the economy. *Scientific American, 263,* 92-99.

Bailey, N.T.J. (1975). *The mathematical theory of infectious diseases and its applications.* London: Charles Griffen. (Original work published in 1957)

Barnett, G.A. (1988). Modeling the diffusion of innovations. In G.A. Barnett & J. Woelfel (Eds.), *Readings in the Galileo system: Theory, methods, and applications* (pp. 55-74). Dubuque, IA: Kendall/Hunt.

Barnett, G.A., Chang, H.J., Fink, E.L., & Richards, W.D. (1991). Seasonality in television viewing: A mathematical model of cultural processes. *Communication Research, 18*(6), 755-772.

Barnett, G.A., Fink, E.L., & Debus, M.B. (1989). A mathematical model of academic citation age. *Communication Research, 16*(4), 510-531.

Bass, F.M. (1969). A new product growth model for consumer durables.

Management Science, 15(5), 215-227.

Beach, L.R., Hope, A., Townes, B., & Campbell, F.L. (1982). the expecta-
    tion-threshold model of reproductive decision making. *Population
    and Environment, 5*(2), 95-108.

Beal, G.M., & Bohlen, J.M. (1955). *How farm people accept new ideas*
    (Report 15). Ames, IA: Cooperative Extension Service.

Beal, G.M., & Rogers, E.M. (1958). The scientist as a referent in the com-
    munication of new technology. *Public Opinion Quarterly, 22*(4),
    555-563.

Becker, M.H. (1970). Sociometric location and innovativeness:
    Reformulation and extension of the diffusion model. *American
    Sociological Review, 35,* 267-282.

Bernard, H.R., Killworth, P., & Sailer, L. (1982). Informant accuracy in
    social network data V. *Social Science Research, 11,* 30-66.

Black, F.L. (1966). Measles endemicity in insular populations: Critical
    community size and its evolutionary implication. *Journal of
    Theoretical Biology, 11,* 07-211.

Bogart, K.P. (1990). *Introductory combinatorics* (2nd ed., pp. 283-309).
    New York: Harcourt Brace Jovanovich.

Boissevain, J. (1974). *Friends of friends: Networks, manipulators and coali-
    tions.* Oxford: Basil Blackwell.

Bolland, J.M. (1988). Sorting out centrality: An analysis of the performance
    of four centrality models in real and simulated networks. *Social
    Networks, 10*(3), 233-253.

Bonacich, P. (1987a). Power and centrality: A family of measures.
    American Journal of Sociology, 92(5), 1170-1182.

Bonacich, P. (1987b). Communication networks and collective action.
    Social Networks, 9, 389-96.

Boorman, S.A., & Levitt, P.R. (1980). *The genetics of altruism.* New York:
    Academic Press.

Boorman, S.A., & White, H.C. (1976). Social structure from multiple net-
    works. II. Role Structures. *American Journal of Sociology, 81*(6),
    1384-1446.

Borgatti, S., Everett, M., & Freeman, L. (1992). *UCINET IV Version 1.0
    Reference Manual.* Columbia, SC: Analytic Technologies.

Brieger, R.L., Boorman, S.A., & Arabie, P. (1975). An algorithm for cluster-
    ing relational data with application to social network analysis and
    comparison with multidimensional scaling. *Journal of Mathematical
    Psychology, 12,* 328-282.

Brown, L.A. (1981). *Innovation diffusion: A new perspective.* New York:
    Methuen.

Brown, L.A., Malecki, E.J., Gross, S.R., Shrestha, M.N., & Semple, R.K.
    (1974). The diffusion of cable television in Ohio: A case study of dif-

fusion agency location patterns and processes of polynuclear type. *Economic Geography, 50*(4), 285-299.

Burt, R.S. (1982). *Toward a structural theory of action: Network models of social structure, perception, and action.* New York: Academic Press.

Burt, R.S. (1987). Social contagion and innovation: Cohesion versus structural equivalence. *American Journal of Sociology, 92,* 1287-1335.

Burt, R.S, & Minor, M. (Eds.). (1983). *Applied network analysis.* Newbury Park, CA: Sage.

Cancian, F. (1979). *The innovator's situation: Uppermiddle-class conservatism in agricultural communities.* Stanford, CA: Stanford University Press.

Caplow, T., & Raymond, J.J. (1954). Factors influencing the selection of pharmaceutical products. *Journal of Marketing, 19,* 18-23.

Carlson, R.O. (1964). School superintendents and the adoption of modern math: A social structure profile. In M. B. Miles (Ed.), *Innovation in education.* New York: Teachers College, Columbia University.

Casetti, E. (1969). Why do diffusion processes conform to logistic trends? *Geographical Analysis, 1*(1), 101-115.

Casetti, E., & Semple R.K. (1969). Concerning the testing of spatial diffusion hypotheses. *Geographical Analysis, 1*(3), 254-259.

Cavalli-Sforza, L.L. (1991, November). Genes, peoples, and languages. *Scientific American,* pp. 104-110.

Ceci, S.J., & Kain, E.L. (1982). Jumping on the bandwagon: The impact of attitude polls on polling behavior. *Public Opinion Quarterly, 46,* 228-242.

Chubin, D. (1976). The conceptualization of scientific specialties. *The Sociological Quarterly, 17,* 448-476.

Coleman, J.S., Katz, E., & Menzel, H. (1966). *Medical innovation: A diffusion study.* New York: Bobbs Merrill.

Coleman, J.S, Menzel, H., & Katz, E. (1957). The diffusion of an innovation among physicians. *Sociometry, 20,* 253-270.

Collins, H.M. (1974). The TEA set: Tacit knowledge and scientific networks. *Science Studies, 4,* 165-186.

Computing Resource Center. (1992). *Stata.* Santa Monica, CA.

Coughenour, C.M. (1965). The problem of reliability of adoption data in survey research. *Rural Sociology, 30,* 184-203.

Crain, R.L. (1966). Fluoridation: The diffusion of an innovation among cities. *Social Forces, 44*(4), 467-476.

Danowski, J.A. (1986). Interpersonal network structure and media use: A focus on radiality and non-mass media use. In G. Gumpert & R. Cathcart (Eds.), *Intermedia* (3rd ed., pp. 168-175). New York: Oxford University Press.

David, P.A. (1985). Clio and the economics of QWERTY. *American Economic Review, 75*(2), 332-337.

Davis, J.A. (1961). Locals and cosmopolitans in American graduate schools. *International Journal of Comparative Sociology, 2*(2), 12-223.

Deutschmann, P.J., & Danielson, W.A. (1960). Diffusion of knowledge of the major news story. *Journalism Quarterly, 37,* 345-355.

Dozier, D.M. (1977). *Communication networks and the role of thresholds in the adoption of innovations.* Unpublished doctoral thesis, Stanford University, Stanford, CA.

Eliason, S.R. (1993). *Maximum likelihood estimation: Logic and practice.* Newbury Park: Sage.

Fine, G.A., & Kleinman, S. (1979). Rethinking subculture: An interactionist analysis. *American Journal of Sociology, 85,* 1-20.

Fischer, C.S. (1978). Urban-to-rural diffusion of opinions in contemporary America. *American Journal of Sociology, 84,* 151-159.

Ford, L.R., & Fulkerson, D.R. (1962). *Flows in networks.* Princeton, NJ: Princeton University Press.

Freeman, L. (1979). Centrality in social networks: Conceptual clarification. *Social Networks, 1,* 215-239.

Freeman, L.C., Borgatti, S.P., & White, D.R. (1991). Centrality in valued graphs: A measure of betweenness based on network flow. *Social Networks, 13,* 141-154.

Friedkin, N. (1982). Information flow through strong and weak ties in intraorganizational social networks. *Social Networks, 3,* 273-285.

Gouldner, A. (1957). Cosmopolitans and locals: Toward an analysis of latent social roles, Part I. *Administrative Science Quarterly, 2,* 282-306.

Gouldner, A. (1958). Cosmopolitans and locals: Toward an analysis of latent social roles, Part II. *Administrative Science Quarterly, 2,* 444-480.

Granovetter, M. (1973). The strength of weak ties. *American Journal of Sociology, 78,* 1360-1380.

Granovetter, M. (1978). Threshold models of collective behavior. *American Journal of Sociology, 83,* 1420-1443.

Granovetter, M. (1982). The strength of weak ties: A network theory revisited. In P.V. Marsden & N. Lin (Eds.), *Social structure and network analysis* (pp. 105-130). Newbury Park: Sage.

Granovetter, M., & Soong, R. (1983). Threshold models of diffusion and collective behavior. *Journal of Mathematical Sociology, 9,* 165-179.

Granovetter, M., & Soong, R. (1986). Threshold models of interpersonal effects in consumer demand. *Journal of Economic Behavior and Organization, 7,* 83-99.

Granovetter, M., & Soong, R. (1988). Threshold models of diversity: Chinese restaurants, residential segregation, and the spiral of silence.

In C.C. Clogg (Ed.), *Sociological methodology* (Vol. 18, pp. 69-104). Washington, DC: American Sociological Association.

Gray, J. (1993). *Men are from Mars, women are from Venus.* New York: Harper Collins.

Greenberg, B. (1964). Person-to-person communication in the diffusion of news events. *Journalism Quarterly, 41*, 489-494.

Greer, A.L. (1977). Advances in the study of diffusion of innovation health care organizations. *Health and Society, 55*(4), 505-532.

Griliches, Z. (1957). Hybrid corn: An exploration in the economics of technical change. *Econometrica, 25*, 501-522.

Guimarães, L. (1972). *Communication integration in modern and traditional social systems: A comparative analysis across twenty communities of Minas Gerais.* Unpublished doctoral thesis, Michigan State University, East Lansing, MI.

Hägerstrand, T. (1967). *Innovation diffusion as a spatial process* (A. Pred, Trans.). Chicago: University of Chicago Press.

Haggett, P. (1976). Hybridizing alternative models of an epidemic diffusion process. *Economic Geography, 52*(2), 136-146.

Hamblin, R.L., Jacobsen, R.B., & Miller, J.L.L. (1973). *A mathematical theory of social change.* New York: John Wiley & Sons.

Harary, F., Norman, R.Z., & Cartwright, D. (1965). *Structural models.* New York: John Wiley & Sons.

Herzog, W.A., Stanfield, J.D., Whiting, G., & Svenning, L. (1968). *Patterns of diffusion in rural Brazil.* Unpublished report, Michigan State University, East Lansing, MI.

Hirschman, A.O. (1972). *Exit voice and loyalty.* New York: Cambridge University Press

Huang, J.C., & Gould, P. (1974). Diffusion in an urban hierarchy: The case of rotary clubs. *Economic Geography, 50*(4), 333-340.

Hudson, J.C. (1969). Diffusion in a central place system. *Geographical Analysis, 1*(1), 45-58.

Hummon, N.P., & Carley, K. (1993). Social networks as normal science. *Social Networks, 15*(1), 71-106.

Inkeles, A. (1968). *Social change in Soviet Russia.* Cambridge, MA: Harvard University Press.

Karlsson, G. (1958). *Social mechanisms: Studies in sociological theory.* New York: The Free Press.

Katz, E. (1957). The two-step flow of communication: An up-to-date report on a hypothesis. *Public Opinion Quarterly, 21*, 61-78.

Katz, E. (1962). The social itinerary of technical change: Two studies on the diffusion of innovation. *Human Organization, 20*, 70-82.

Katz, E., & Lazarsfeld, P. (1955). *Personal influence: The part played by people in the flow of mass communications.* New York: The Free Press.

Katz, E., Levine, M.L., & Hamilton, H. (1963). Traditions of research on the diffusion of innovation. *American Sociological Review, 28*, 237-253.

Katz, M.L., & Shapiro, C. (1986). Technology adoption in the presence of network externalities. *Journal of Political Economy, 94*(4), 822-841.

Kerckhoff, A., & Back, K. (1968). *The June Bug: A study of hysterical contagion.* New York: Appleton-Century-Crofts.

Kerckhoff, A., Back, K., & Miller, N. (1965). Sociometric patterns in hysterical contagion. *Sociometry, 28*, 2-15.

Kermack, W.O., & McKendrick, A.G. (1927). A contribution to the mathematical theory of epidemics. *Journal of the Royal Society of London, A115*, 700-721.

Killworth, P., Bernard, H.R., & McCarty, C. (1984). Measuring patterns of acquaintanceship. *Current Anthropology, 25*(4), 381-397.

Kincaid, D.L., Das Gupta, A., Mitra, S.N., Whitney, E., Senior, M., Yun, S.H., & Massiah, E. (1993). *Community networks and family planning promotion: Impact of the "Jiggasha" approach in Trishal, Bangladesh.* Paper presented at the annual meeting of the American Public Health Association, San Francisco.

King, L.J. (1984) *Central place theory.* Newbury Park, CA: Sage.

Knoke, D., & Kuklinski, J. H. (1982). *Network analysis.* Newbury Park, CA: Sage.

Krackhardt, D., & Porter, L. (1986). The snowball effect: Turnover embedded in communication networks. *Journal of Applied Psychology, 71*, 50-55.

Krassa, M.A. (1988). Social groups, selective perception, and behavioral contagion in public opinion. *Social Networks, 10*, 109-136.

Kuran, T. (1987). Preference falsification, policy continuity and collective conservatism. *The Economic Journal, 97*, 642-665.

Kuran, T. (1989). Sparks and prairie fires: A theory of anticipated political revolution. *Public Choice, 61*, 41-74.

Lang, K., & Lang, G.E. (1984). The impact of polls on public opinion. *Annals of the American Academy of Political and Social Science, 472*, 129-142.

Lee, S.B. (1977). *System effects on family planning innovativeness in Korean villages.* Unpublished doctoral thesis, University of Michigan, Ann Arbor, MI.

Lin, N., Dayton, P.W., & Greenwald, P. (1977). The urban communication network and social stratification: A "small world experiment." In B.D. Ruben (Ed.), *Communication yearbook* (Vol. 1, pp. 107-119). New Brunswick, NJ: Transaction Books.

Lorrain, F., & White, H.C. (1971). Structural equivalence of individuals in social networks. *Journal of Mathematical Sociology, 1*, 49-80.

Macy, M.W. (1990). Learning theory and the logic of critical mass. *American Sociological Review, 55*, 809-826.

Macy, M.W. (1991). Chains of cooperation: Threshold effects in collective action. *American Sociological Review, 56*, 730-747.

Mahajan, V., & Peterson, R.A. (1985). *Models of innovation diffusion*. Newbury Park, CA: Sage.

Markus, M.L. (1987). Toward a "critical mass" theory of interactive media: Universal access, interdependence and diffusion. *Communication Research, 14*(5), 491-511.

Markus, M.L. (1990). Toward a "critical mass" theory of interactive media. In J. Fulk & C. Steinfield (Eds.), *Organizations and communication technology* (pp. 194-217). Newbury Park, CA: Sage.

Marsden, P.V. (1990). Network data and measurement. *Annual Review of Sociology, 16*, 435-463.

Marsden, P.V., & Podolny, J. (1990). Dynamic analysis of network diffusion processes. In J. Weesie & H. Flap (Eds.), *Social networks through time*. Utrecht: ISOR.

Marwell, G., Oliver, P., & Prahl, R. (1988). Social networks and collective action: A theory of the critical mass. III. *American Journal of Sociology, 94*, 503-534.

McCombs, M.E., & Shaw, D.L. (1972). The agenda-setting function of the mass media. *Public Opinion Quarterly, 36*, 176-187.

Mellot, J.L. (1990). GNET. Pittsburgh: University of Pittsburgh.

Menzel, H. (1960). Innovation, integration, and marginality: A survey of physicians. *American Sociological Review, 25*, 704-713.

Menzel, H., & Katz, E. (1955). Social relations and innovation in the medical profession: The epidemiology of a new drug. *Public Opinion Quarterly, 19*, 337-352.

Merton, R.K. (1968). Patterns of influence: Local and cosmopolitan influentials. In R.K. Merton (Ed.), *Social theory and social structure* (pp. 441-474). New York: Free Press.

Microsoft. (1991). *Excel*. Redmond, WA: Author.

Milgram, S. (1967). The small world problem. *Psychology Today, 1*, 62-67.

Monin, J.P., Benayoun, R., & Sert, B. (1976). *Initiation to the mathematics of the processes of diffusion, contagion, and propagation* (M. Brandon, Trans.). The Hague; Mouton.

Moody Blues. (1969). *The threshold of a dream*. London: Epigram Records.

Morrill, R., Gaile, G.L., & Thrall, G.I. (1988). *Spatial diffusion*. Newbury Park: CA. Sage.

Moscovici, S. (1976). *Social influence and social change* (C. Sherrard & G. Heinz, Trans.). New York: Academic Press.

Navazio, R. (1977). An experimental approach to bandwagon research. *Public Opinion Quarterly, 41*(2), 217-225.

Neuman, W.R. (1990) The threshold of public attention. *Public Opinion Quarterly, 54*, 159-176.

Nischan, P., Ebeling, K., Thomas, D.B., & Hirsch, U. (1993). Comparison of recalled and validated oral contraceptive histories. *American Journal of Epidemiology, 138*(9), 697-703.

Noelle-Neumann, E. (1977). Turbulences in the climate of opinion: Methodological applications of the spiral of silence theory. *Public Opinion Quarterly, 41*, 143-158.

Noelle-Neumann, E. (1984). *The spiral of silence.* Chicago: University of Chicago Press.

O'Gorman, H., & Garry, S. (1976). Pluralistic ignorance: A replication and extension. *Public Opinion Quarterly, 40*, 449-458.

Oliver, P.E., & Marwell, G. (1988). The paradox of group size in collective action: A theory of the critical mass. II. *American Sociological Review, 53*, 1-8.

Oliver, P.E., Marwell, G., & Teixeira, R. (1985). A theory of the critical mass. I. interdependence, group heterogeneity, and the production of collective action. *American Journal of Sociology, 91*(3), 522-56.

Olson, M. (1965). *The logic of collective action.* New York: Schocken Books.

Oren, S.S., & Smith, S.A. (1981). Critical mass and tariff structure in electronic communications markets. *Bell Journal of Economics, 12*, 467-487.

Panko, R.R. (1988). *Discretion and skewed use in computer-supported cooperative work (CSCW).* IFIP Working Group on Organizations and Information Systems. Working Conference on Desktop Information Technology, Cornell University, Ithaca, NY.

Park, H.J., Chung, K.K., Han, D.S., & Lee, S.B. (1974). *Mothers' clubs and family planning in Korea.* Seoul, Korea: School of Public Health, Seoul National University.

Pederson, P.O. (1970). Innovation diffusion within and between national urban systems. *Geographical Analysis, 2*(3), 203-254.

Pemberton, E. (1936). The curve of culture diffusion rate. *American Sociological Review, 1*, 547-556.

Pemberton, E. (1937). The effect of a social crisis on the curve of diffusion. *American Sociological Review, 2*(1), 55-61.

Prahl, R., Marwell, G., & Oliver, P. (1991). Reach and selectivity as strategies of recruitment for collective action: A theory of the critical mass V. *Journal of Mathematical Sociology, 16*(2), 137-164.

Price, V., & Allen, S. (1990). Opinion spirals, silent and otherwise: Applying small-group research to public opinion. *Communication Research, 17*(3), 369-392.

Pyle, G.F. (1969). The diffusion of cholera in the United States in the nineteenth century. *Geographical Analysis, 1*(1), 59-75.

Rapoport, A., & Horvath, W.J. (1961). A study of a large sociogram. *Behavioral Science, 6*(4), 279-291.

Ray, D.M., Villeneuve, P.Y., & Roberge, R.A. (1974). Functional prerequisites, spatial diffusion, and allometric growth. *Economic Geography, 50*(4), 341-351.

Renfrew, C. (1989). The origins of Indo-European languages. *Scientific American, 261*(4), 106-114.

Rice, R.E. (1982). Longitudinal role development and system structure or researchers using a computer conferencing system. In M. Burgoon (Ed.), *Communication yearbook* (Vol. 6). Newbury Park, CA: Sage.

Rice, R.E. (1990). Computer-mediated communication system network data: Theoretical concerns and empirical examples. *International Journal of Man-Machine Studies, 32,* 627-647.

Rice, R.E. (1993). Using network concepts to clarify sources and mechanisms of social influence. In W.D. Richards & G.A. Barnett (Eds.), *Progress in communication sciences* (Vol XII, pp. 44-62). Norwood, NJ: Ablex.

Rice, R.E., & Aydin, C. (1991). Attitudes toward new organizational technology: Network proximity as a mechanism for social information processing. *Administrative Science Quarterly, 36,* 219-244.

Rice, R.E., Grant, A., Schmitz, J., & Torobin, J. (1990). Individual and network influences on the adoption and perceived outcomes of electronic messaging. *Social Networks, 12,* 1-29.

Richards, W.D. (1989). *The NEGOPY network analysis program.* Vancouver, Canada: Department of Communication, Simon Fraser University.

Robinson, J.P. (1976). Interpersonal influence in election campaigns: Two step-flow hypotheses. *Public Opinion Quarterly, 40,* 304-319.

Rogers, E.M. (1962). *Diffusion of innovations.* New York: Free Press.

Rogers, E.M. (1983). *Diffusion of innovations.* New York: The Free Press.

Rogers, E.M., Ascroft, J.R., & Röling, N. (Eds.). (1970). *Diffusion of innovations in Brazil, Nigeria, and India.* Unpublished report, Michigan State University, East Lansing, MI.

Rogers, E.M., & Beal, G.M. (1958). The importance of personal influence in adoption of technological changes. *Social Forces, 36*(4), 329-334.

Rogers, E.M., & Cartano, D.G. (1962). Methods of measuring opinion leadership. *Public Opinion Quarterly, 26,* 435-441.

Rogers, E.M., & Kincaid, D.L. (1981). *Communication networks: A new paradigm for research.* New York: Free Press.

Rogers, E.M. & Shoemaker, F.F. (1971). *Communication of innovations: A cross-cultural approach.* New York: Free Press.

Rohlfs, J. (1974). A theory of interdependent demand for a communications service. *Bell Journal of Economics and Management Science, 5,* 16-37.

Ryan, R., & Gross, N. (1943). The diffusion of hybrid seed corn in two Iowa communities. *Rural Sociology, 8*(1), 15-24.

Ryan, R., & Gross, N. (1950). *Acceptance and diffusion of hybrid corn seed in two Iowa communities, Rural Sociology* (Research Bulletin 372). Ames: Iowa Agricultural Experiment Station.

Sailer, L.D. (1978). Structural equivalence: Meaning and definition, computation and application. *Social Networks, 1,* 73-90.

Schelling, T. (1978). *Micromotives & macrobehavior.* New York: Norton.

Scott, J. (1991). *Network analysis: A handbook.* Newbury Park, CA: Sage.

Shorrett, J. (1983). *A threshold model for adoption of home health innovations.* Unpublished doctoral thesis, University of Michigan, Ann Arbor, MI.

SNAPS (Social Network Analysis Procedures for Gauss, Version 1.0). (1989). Santa Barbara: Noah E. Friedkin, University of California at Santa Barbara.

Stephenson, K., & Zelen, M. (1989). Rethinking centrality: Methods and examples. *Social Networks, 11*(1), 1-37.

Stern, L.W., Craig, C.S., La Greca, A.J., & Salem, R.G. (1976). The effect of sociometric location on the adoption of an innovation within a university faculty. *Sociology of Education, 49,* 90-96.

Strang, D. (1990). From dependency to sovereignty: An event history analysis of decolonization 1870-1987. *American Sociological Review, 55,* 846-860.

Strang, D. (1991). Adding social structure to diffusion models: An event history framework. *Sociological Methods and Research, 19,* 324-353.

STRUCTURE. (1989a). STRUCTURE: A general purpose network analysis program (Version 4.1 Command Booklet). New York: Research Program in Structural Analysis, Center for the Social Sciences, Columbia University.

STRUCTURE. (1989b). STRUCTURE ASSISTANT (Version 2.0 Command Booklet). New York: Research Program in Structural Analysis, Center for the Social Sciences, Columbia University.

Tannen, D. (1993). *You just don't understand: Men and women in conversation.* New York: Ballantine Books.

Taylor, D.G. (1982). Pluralistic ignorance and the spiral of silence: A formal analysis. *Public Opinion Quarterly, 46,* 311-335.

Teachman, J.D., & Hayward, M.D. (1993). Interpreting hazard rate models. *Sociological Methods and Research, 21*(3), 340-371.

Travers, J., & Milgram, S. (1969). An experimental study of the "small-world" problem. *Sociometry, 32,* 425-443.

Tuma, N.B., & Hannan, M.T. (1984). *Social dynamics: Models and methods.* New York: Academic Press.

Valente, T.W. (1993). Diffusion of innovations and policy decision-making. *Journal of Communication, 43*(1), 30-41.

Valente, T.W. & Bardini, T. (1994). Virtual diffusion or an uncertain reality: Networks, policy and models for the diffusion of VR technology. In F. Biocca &* M. Levy (Eds.), *Communication in the age of virtual reality* (pp. 308-322). Northvale, NJ: Erlbaum.

Valente, T.W., Kim, Y.M., Lettenmaier, C., Glass, W., & Dibba, Y. (1994). Radio and the promotion of family planning in The Gambia. *International Family Perspectives Planning, 20*(3), 96-100.

Weimann, G. (1982). On the importance of marginality: One more step into the two-step flow of communication. *American Sociological Review, 47,* 764-773.

Wellman, B. (1983). Network analysis: Some basic principles. in R. Collins (Ed.), *Sociological theory* (pp. 155-200). San Francisco: Jossey-Bass.

White, H.C., Boorman, S.A., & Breiger, R.L. (1976). Social structure from multiple networks. I. Blockmodels of roles and positions. *American Journal of Sociology, 81*(4), 730-780.

Whittle, P. (1955). The outcome of a stochastic epidemic-A note on Bailey's paper. *Biometrika, 42,* 116-122.

⸻ Author Index ⸻

═══Subject Index═══